ḤUSAYN

A Symbol and a Warning

ḤUSAYN

A Symbol and a Warning

ESSAYS BY

Muhammad Iqbal

Abul Kalam Azad

Zakir Ḥusain Khan

Abul Alā Mawdūdī

Compiled and translated from
Persian and Urdu into English by

Mohd ʿAbd al-Rahman Sayeed Siddiqi

Islamic Book Trust

Published by
Islamic Book Trust
607 Mutiara Majestic
Jalan Othman
46000 Petaling Jaya
Selangor, Malaysia
www.ibtbooks.com

Islamic Book Trust is affiliated with The Other Press.

Perpustakaan Negara Malaysia Cataloguing-in-Publication Data

Husayn : A Symbol and a Warning / Essays by Muhammad Iqbal, Abul Kalam Azad, Zakir Husain Khan, Abul Ala Mawdudi ; Compiled and translated from Persian and Urdu into English by Mohd 'Abd al-Rahman Sayeed Siddiqi.
ISBN 978-967-0526-85-0
eISBN 978-967-0526-86-7
1. Husayn ibn 'Ali, -680. 2. Islam--History.
3. Karbala, Battle of, Karbala', Iraq, 680.
I. Abul Kalam Azad. II. Zakir Husain Khan.
III. Abul Ala Mawdudi. IV. Mohd 'Abd al-Rahman Sayeed Siddiqi.
V. Title.
297.0902

Printed by
SS Graphic Printers (M) Sdn. Bhd.
Lot 7 & 8, Jalan TIB 3
Taman Industri Bolton
68100 Batu Caves, Selangor

Contents

Publisher's Note

Hitherto our understanding has been that there is no disagreement between Shias and Sunnis that Imam Ḥusayn's martyrdom in Karbala was a historical event illustrating true Islamic leadership and the exemplary character of someone who made a sincere attempt at safeguarding the ideology of Islam with the intention to retain it as an exact replica of the setup of the Prophetic era. But of late we see attempts by some Wahabis to make Ḥusayn's martyrdom a Sunni-Shia polemic, so much so that it was astonishing to see a Wahabi "scholar" have the temerity to absolve Mu'āwiya and his son and successor Yazīd from all responsibility for this heinous crime of Ḥusayn's murder and to put the blame on Ḥusayn himself. According to him this happened because Ḥusayn ignored "wise" advice from his elders when all odds were against him and was adamant in asserting his claim to the caliphate when affairs of the Islamic state were running smoothly under the new system of kingship.

The hero of this great event is not only the scion of the most sacred family, nor do his life and martyrdom provide an occasion for only mourning and tears. Rather, they infuse in believers a fervent desire for sacrifice and illuminate the existing system of life with the beacon of truth and justice. Thus it may be seen how Ḥusayn's performance is intimately associated with the collective life of the Muslim community. This is the essence of the story that deserves our attention.

At first we planned to republish a booklet containing four essays on Karbala by four highly respected Sunni scholars and leaders, but added a new essay to expand the story and give the reader a more comprehensive understanding of the importance of this heart-rending tragedy in Islamic history. For want of a better title, we added the article as a foreword to this book.

The first selection is not an essay but a famous Persian poem entitled "The Secret of the Karbala Event" from *Secrets of Selflessness* by the great twentieth-century Indian poet and interpreter of Islamic thought Dr. Muhammad Iqbal. The poem is of paramount importance in Islamic literature. In view of this fact, the Persian text has also been published along with the English translation so that those interested may receive full inspiration from it.

Next appears a selection from Abul Kalam Azad's writings on this subject, excellently chosen and arranged in its authentic historical context together with his scholarly deductions. Azad was one of the most prominent leaders of the Indian freedom struggle, as well as an author, a commentator and the first education minister of independent India. He conveyed his views through his periodicals, *Al-Hilal* and *Al-Balagh*, and the programme formulated for the organisation styled as Hizbullah.

The third piece is an old article by the distinguished scholar and former president of the Indian Republic Dr. Zakir Husain Khan. It is a work of universal appeal with a philosophical tinge, and a literary masterpiece.

The last of the four articles is from Abul Alā Mawdūdī, who, in the words of Wilfred Cantwell Smith, is "the most systematic thinker of modern Islam". To his credit are numerous works, which cover "a range of disciplines such as Qur'anic exegesis, *ḥadīth*, law, philosophy and history". If one wishes to know about the goal of Ḥusayn's caravan and how to keep its track, the Mawdūdī's thought-provoking article would give him a correct lead. Ḥusayn's sacrifice is as clear as daylight.

All the above four essays were compiled and translated from Persian and Urdu into English by Mr. Mohd. 'Abd al-Rahman Sayeed Siddiqi. Mr. Sayeed also wrote a well-researched introduction, which is also included as an introduction to the essays in this book.

Islamic Book Trust
Kuala Lumpur, Malaysia
December 2020

The Eternal Meaning of Imam Ḥusayn's Martyrdom

Prof. Abdulaziz Sachedina,
George Mason University[1]

The purpose behind studying the historical events that led to the martyrdom of Imam Ḥusayn in the year 61/680 is, primarily, to try to articulate intelligibly the humanly most significant questions that have since altered the context of routine human life in Islamic history. As such, what happened in that year cannot remain just private concern with the past, because the events at Karbala, Iraq, were in some sense or other outstanding in the context of humankind generally, and not just in relation to the Prophet's ﷺ family or their adherents. The day of 'Āshūrā has proven to be an event with obvious religious and moral implications whose significance is universally perceived and whose religious and moral challenges cannot be ignored by anyone who claims to be a Muslim. The religious and moral deeds that took place on this day have remained unrepeatable ones that have an everlasting claim to our respect. After having known those deeds, the Muslim community can never remain indifferent to the Islamic challenges posed by the event of Karbala, not because of the tragic nature of those deeds, but because those deeds cause spiritual and moral awareness and motivation in us and add to our understanding of who we are and of what we are committed to both as human beings and Muslims. Furthermore, the events of Karbala generate in us a sense of what is worthy of our wonder and our tears.

Hence, the study of the events in Karbala ought to revive in us the great commitment and loyalty that we, as Muslims, have borne towards the Islamic revelation—the commitment and loyalty made explicit by the events on the day of 'Āshūrā, when the male and female, the old and young members and supporters of the Prophet's ﷺ family demonstrated the excellence of their human endeavour. In the final analysis, it is the relevance of Karbala to humanity that continues to challenge our conceptions of standards of human respect and recognition for as long as there remain conscientious beings on earth.

However, Imam Ḥusayn's struggle to uphold the spiritual and moral values of Islam becomes comprehensible when seen in the light of the entire struggle of Abrahamic traditions to assert the oneness of God (*tawḥīd*). In other words, the assertion of monotheism, which is pre-eminently attributed to Abraham in the Qur'an (Yūsuf 12:37-40), calls for the act of submitting to God (Islam), which means accepting a spiritual and moral responsibility to uphold the standards of action held to have God's authority. Hence, accepting Islam and its challenge meant that Muslims opened themselves to vast new considerations of what life might mean when a person "submits" to God. So construed, their act of "submission" could be defined as commitment to the Abrahamic faith enunciated by Prophet Muḥammad ﷺ, which is required to establish an intensely creative person as committed to the social and juridical consequences of being a Muslim. Consequently, adherence to Islam presented an opportunity to build a new order of social life such as the Islamic vision had more and more obviously demanded. The "submission" to God demanded, in the first place, a personal devotion to spiritual and moral purity; but personal piety and purity implied a just social behaviour. Sooner or later, this challenge of Abrahamic faith was bound to require the creation of just social order as the natural outgrowth and context of the personal piety and purity (*taqwā*) it required, because Islam is never satisfied with mere exposition of its ideals, but constantly seeks the means to implement them. Obviously, when no Muslim could have remained neutral to this challenge of Islam, how could Imam Ḥusayn have tolerated a movement spearheaded by the Umayyads that attacked the ideals and principles of Islamic social order and suggested an alternative sort of sanction for their behaviour and especially for social leadership?

It is therefore pertinent to understand Imam Ḥusayn's revolution within the historical context created by the individual's relationship to God and maintained by the aspirations for the creation of just public order prevalent in the Muslim community as a whole and given form in their corporate life. By regarding the events of Karbala as subordinate, some Muslim scholars, and following them, some Westerners, have tried to reduce the exceptional significance of the struggle of Imam Ḥusayn and its impact on the course of subsequent Islamic history. Undoubtedly, without full reference to the general socio-political milieu that developed following the death of the Prophet ﷺ in the year 632, and that culminated in the events of Karbala, the day of 'Āshūrā appears to be a mere tragedy without any meaning and significance for posterity. Imam Ḥusayn's revolution cannot be isolated from the general historical context of the Islamic challenge, within which he and his followers acted to make the purpose of the revolution explicit. In other words, it is impossible to appreciate the purpose behind Imam Ḥusayn's and his followers' martyrdoms without first understanding the historical circumstances that called on him to defend the spiritual and moral heritage of Islam.

This is indeed a difficult task, because it is usually considered an impossible undertaking to separate two consecutive events in the history of human society. The explanation of this difficulty lies in the gradual nature of change of factors that demarcate one historical period from another. Moreover, it is even more difficult to demarcate the end of one period of a society and the beginning of another when two consecutive periods are required to be examined in order to determine the subsequent changes. It is this difficulty adumbrated in sensitive consequences to one's cherished notions about a particular period in Islamic history, especially the early days following the death of the Prophet ﷺ, which has caused Muslim scholars in general to deviate from the responsibility of preserving their scholarly integrity in treating the history of Imam Ḥusayn. Thus the imperative need to properly demarcate the period when the Muslim community began to witness their leaders' obvious deviation from the fundamental teachings of Islam, in order to fully discuss Imam Ḥusayn's response, has been ignored by many Muslim historians. It is only through objective evaluation of the early period of Islamic history that it becomes possible to understand the stance Imam Ḥusayn took in the year 60-61/679-80. However, for a number of Muslim historians, who have generally failed to point out the obvious deviations from the Islamic revelation in the period that followed the Prophet's ﷺ death, the challenge lies in revising their tendentious—historical presentation of that early period, which has been slow in coming forth. Nevertheless, a consensus among all historians[2] belonging to various schools of Muslim thought has emerged that it is possible, at least, to fix the period of these deviations from Islamic norms, if not earlier, then, from the beginning of the second half of the period of 'Uthmān's caliphate (644-656 AD).

'Uthmān's caliphate typifies a period that caused general political and religious patterns to drift away from the standards that were provided by Islam.

Indeed, it became apparent that the new currents in the Muslim community around this period that went towards creating new forms in the realm of public order were the result of these currents interacting with the mentality of the group that held power in the society, namely, the Umayyads, who had very little concern for the ideals of Islam. As a result, it is not sufficient merely to discuss these new forms at that time limiting ourselves to the evaluation of the external forms only; rather, it is necessary to embark on a serious discussion of the factors that created these forms and the way they affected the society and the personages who moulded the history of this period. Such inquiry remains legitimate public concern, which puts the event of 'Āshūrā in its proper perspective. The main question, then, that we intend to treat is: What had happened to Islam during this period that Imam Ḥusayn felt it necessary to take on himself to undo the harm the Umayyads were causing to it?

Islam conceives of human nature in terms of both its spiritual and physical needs, and as such it is never content with mere exposition of its ideals, but constantly seeks the means to implement them. The Qur'an gave Muslims every reason to wish for a government and a society that would be based on the noble paradigm set by the political and the ideal sides of the Prophet's ﷺ mission on earth. However, major political undertakings of the early Muslim leaders inevitably demonstrated a lack of commitment to the noble paradigm. Since 'Uthmān's time, the ruling class had used Islam more or less as a badge of identity. Whereas Islamic ideals carried a responsible and egalitarian social commitment, these rulers were engaged in creating a privileged class of a small elite tied together by common Arab heritage. The implications of such a deviation from the Islamic ideal became discernible to those Muslims who were most serious about the moral and political responsibilities that an acceptance of the Islamic faith entailed. The most obvious implication of reference to the Arabic heritage in ordering public and private life meant that Islam became the envied badge of a favoured ruling class of Arabs who happened to be bound together by Islam. As such, that would have made Islam an Ishmaelism (as the Arabs were the descendants of Ishmael, the son of Abraham), analogous to the Israelism of the Jews, in which converts could enter as members of the community only on the basis of their having descended from Abraham. Despite the comprehensiveness of the Islamic ideal and its universalistic direction, the exalting of the Arabs as being of the line of Ishmael and producing an ethnically-bound community became part of the political program of the Umayyads from the second half of 'Uthmān's caliphate. The most important consequence of this political mission, which gradually became clearer, was that Muslims were not treated on an equal basis as prescribed by the Qur'anic dictum regarding the "brotherhood of all believers", and the Prophet's ﷺ recommendation to the Muslims to renounce all conflict based on genealogy. On the contrary, the great families of Medina who descended from the Prophet's ﷺ close associates were accorded "social priority" (*tafdil*), and the sense of the inviolability of the Arab tribesmen was reinforced against the Qur'anic requirement that a Muslim, regardless of his ethnic affiliation, had to be accorded that personal liberty and dignity.

Consistent with this anti-egalitarian attitude of the early Muslim leaders was the development of elaborate forms of urban luxury and social distinction. The fruits of conquest, in the form of the booty and the revenue from the conquered lands, had created an unequal distribution of wealth among all Arab Muslims. Consequently, the wealth was concentrated among the conquering families, affording them privileges based on arbitrary distinctions of rank. According to al-Dhahabī, during 'Uthmān's reign there was so much wealth in Medina that a horse would sell for a hundred thousand *dirhams*, while a garden would fetch four hundred thousand. The Umayyads, says al-Dhahabī, had, during this period, acted indiscriminately in amassing wealth to the extent that they had discredited the caliphate as the guarantor of the equality of all Muslims in sharing the wealth acquired through the spoils and the taxes from the conquered lands. Muʿāwiya, who symbolises the prevailing tendencies of the Arab aristocracy in the first century of Islam, clearly formed his policies as the Arab chief, concerned perhaps less with the directives of the Qur'an or the Prophetic "pattern of moral behaviour"—the *Sunnah*. It can be maintained with much documentation that the Umayyad rulers did the minimum for the consolidation of Islamic matters. The Umayyad rulers and their governors—who were by and large neither pious nor committed to Islam—were not the people to promote a religious and social life corresponding to the *Sunnah* of the Prophet ﷺ. As a matter of fact, reference to the *Sunnah* was not necessarily a reference to the *Sunnah* of the Prophet ﷺ; rather, Muʿāwiya made frequent references to the *Sunnah* of ʿUmar in setting the fiscal policies of the state. There was little concern about the religious life of the population. As true Arabs, they paid little attention to religion, either in their own conduct or in that of their subjects. If a man was observant of his religious obligation and was seen to be devoutly worshiping in the mosque, it was assumed that he was not a follower of the Umayyad dynasty, but an ardent supporter of ʿAlī.

Individual examples cited by several authoritative traditionalists indicate the state of affairs in regard to the ignorance prevailing among the Umayyads about the ritual performances and religious precepts in the first century. In Syria, where the Umayyads had the staunchest support, it was not generally known that there were only five canonical daily prayers, and in order to make certain of this fact, it was decided that an associate of the Prophet ﷺ who was still alive should be asked about it. It is impossible to fully comprehend the state of affairs that prevailed under the Umayyads when the rulers of the people who lived under them showed very little concern for the understanding of the laws and rules of Islam, Indeed, such a period was alluded to in the Prophetic tradition that predicted the critical religious future of the Muslim community:

> "There will come rulers after me who will destroy the canonical prayers (*ṣalāh*) but continue to perform the prayers at the fixed times all the same."

Moreover, the Umayyad hatred of the Hashemites, especially the Prophet's ﷺ family, which was evident under Mu'āwiya and his successors, give rise to controversies among Muslims on issues of Islam, whether political or doctrinal. The Umayyad spirit of fabrication, dissemination and suppression of Prophetic traditions is evident in the instruction Mu'āwiya gave to his governor al-Mughīra on defaming 'Alī and his companions:

> "Do not tire of abusing and insulting 'Alī and calling for God's mercifulness for 'Uthmān, defaming the companions of 'Alī, removing them, and refusing to listen to them, praising, in contrast, the clan of 'Uthmān, drawing them near to you, and listening to them."

This instruction is in the form of official encouragement to fabricate lies directed against 'Alī and to hold back and suppress those reports that favoured him. Evidently, the Umayyads and their political followers had no scruples in promoting tendentious lies in the form of Prophetic traditions, and they were prepared to cover such falsifications with their undoubted authority.

One such pious authority was al-Zuhrī, who could not resist pressure from the governing authorities, and was willing to promote the interests of the Umayyad dynasty by religious means. Al-Zuhrī belonged to the circle of those Muslims who believed that a *modus vivendi* with the Umayyad government was desirable. However, even he could not cover up the report that Anas ibn Mālik had related regarding the critical religious situation under the Umayyads. The report is preserved in *Ṣaḥīḥ al-Bukhārī*, in a section entitled "Not offering the prayer at its stated time":

> "Al-Zuhrī relates that he visited Anas ibn Mālik in Damascus and found him weeping, and asked him the reason for his weeping. He replied 'I do not know anything I used to know during the lifetime of the Messenger of God (everything is lost) except this prayer (*ṣalāh*) which (too) is being lost (that is, not being offered as it should be).'"

That the manner in which this well-established Prophetic practice of prayer had been altered, either out of ignorance or due to the anti-*Sunna*h and anti-'Alī attitude of the Umayyads, is further demonstrated by another tradition in *al-Bukhārī*, in the section entitled "To end the *takbir* (saying "God is greater") on prostrating". The tradition is narrated on the authority of Mutarrif ibn 'Abd Allāh, who said:

> "'Imran ibn Ḥusain and I offered the prayer behind 'Alī ibn Abī Ṭālib (in Basra). When 'Alī prostrated, he said the *takbir*, when he raised his head he said the *takbir*, and when he stood up for the third unit (*rak'a*) he said the *takbir*. On the completion of the prayer, 'Imran took my hand and said, 'He ('Alī) made me remember the prayer of Muḥammad, on whom be peace.' Or he said (something to the effect that) 'He led us in a prayer like that of Muḥammad, on whom be peace.'"

The above facts show sufficiently the prevailing trend in the Umayyad state, where Islam was above all a badge of united Arab aristocracy, the code and discipline of a conquering elite. As would become apparent in subsequent periods, the traditions of Arab aristocracy had relatively little inherent connection with Islam itself. In fact, under the Umayyads a responsible and egalitarian spirit of Islam was ignored in favour of power politics. Under such circumstances, the faithful had to deal with a crucial moral and religious question: To what extent could the Muslims consent to obey the rulers, who were completely opposed to the basic teachings of Islam?

It is possible to surmise from various sources on

this period of Islamic history that the Umayyads presented a dilemma for the committed Muslims as to how they were to order their religious life under such rulers. Of course, there were some, like al-Zuhrī, who did not consider the deviation from the religious obligations by the Umayyads a sufficient reason to refuse obedience to them and declare them as unjust. These were the Murjites, who believed that to acknowledge the Umayyads as true believers it was sufficient that they professed Islam outwardly, and that it was not necessary to pry into their un-Islamic behaviour. Accordingly, these people did not raise any objection to the cruel measures adopted by the Umayyads and their governors against those pious individuals like Ḥujr ibn ʿAdī and, later on, Imam Ḥusayn, who refused them their allegiance on the basis of their conviction that as an essential consequence of their religious responsibility they could not do so. On the contrary, the Murjites even defended the massacre the Umayyads caused among their most pious opponents on the grounds that these individuals were disrupting the unity of the community by challenging the authority that represented the Muslim community as a whole.

There were others among the pious people, who, although acknowledging the unworthiness of the Umayyads to rule the community on religious grounds, maintained that the *de facto* rule of the Umayyads was in the interest of the state and of Islamic unity. They thereby contributed towards the acceptance of the rulers, and the people, following their lead, tolerated and paid allegiance to the un-Islamic regime. Furthermore, the accommodating outlook of this group laid the groundwork for the acceptance of any claim to legitimacy by a Muslim authority that managed to successfully seize power through upheaval or revolution.

On the other hand, we have people like Imam Ḥusayn, who refused to acknowledge these corrupt leaders and their representatives at all, and met them with resistance. As such, Imam Ḥusayn and his followers provide a clear contrast to accommodation to Umayyad policies. Imam Ḥusayn's unbending religious attitude stems from his conviction about the political responsibilities that an acceptance of Islamic revelation entailed.

In his letter to the people of Kufa, who had urged him to come to Iraq to assume the responsibilities of an imam, he reaffirms his penetrating awareness of the religio-political responsibilities of the imam. He says:

> "I solemnly declare that a person is not the imam if he does not act in accordance with the

> Book (of God), and does not follow justice (in dealing with the people), and is not subject to the truth, and does not devote himself entirely to God."

Undoubtedly, one can discern the implication of the above statement in Imam Ḥusayn's declaration, made in a speech to the army of Hurr, who had come to intercept him on his way to Iraq. This declaration shows the disgust of the pious with the life lived under the ungodly Umayyads:

> "Do you not see that truth is not followed anymore, and that falsehood is not being interdicted [by anyone]? Indeed, it is within the rights of a believer to desire to meet God. Verily, I do not see death except [in the form of] martyrdom; and I do not see life with the unjust as anything but loathsome."

It is evident that Imam Ḥusayn was reacting to the general condition of deterioration in the upholding of the Islamic teaching brought about by the anti-religious Umayyads and the prevailing outlook of accommodation among the Muslims encouraged by those theologians who supported the existing order and wanted to prevent civil strife at the expense of the Qur'anic principle of justice. Thus, the events of the year 1680 become comprehensible when seen in light of the Qur'anic insistence on the establishment of a just social order under the guidance provided by God in the form of the Book and the "noble paradigm" of the Prophet ﷺ, and the manner in which the representatives of the Muslim community deviated from this goal following the death of the Prophet ﷺ. Moreover, it was the commitment to the ideals of Islam that finally decided the course adopted by Imam Ḥusayn and his followers in Karbala on the day of 'Āshūrā—a day that continues and will continue to challenge our conceptions of standards of human respect and recognition for as long as there remains a conscientious being on earth.

It is, I believe, the message of truth and justice—the Islamic revelation in its entirety—that makes the study and the commemoration of Imam Ḥusayn's martyrdom deserving of our wonder and our tears. In Islamic history there is no other occasion that can generate the total responsibility that a Muslim has towards God and his fellow men. Furthermore, there is no other "paradigm" that equals the paradigm provided by all the members of the Prophet's ﷺ family in creating an egalitarian social commitment, which Islam obviously demands from its adherents. It is this paradigmatic nature of Imam Ḥusayn's life that gives it an eternal meaning, promised in the Qur'an, to all those who struggle and sacrifice their lives in the cause of God:

> "*Count not those who are slain in God's way as dead, but rather as living with their Lord, by Him provided.*" (Āl 'Imrān 3:169)

Notes

[1] Abdulaziz Sachedina, Ph.D., is Professor and IIIT Chair in Islamic Studies at George Mason University in Fairfax, Virginia. Dr. Sachedina, who has studied in India, Iraq, Iran and Canada, obtained his Ph.D. from the University of Toronto. He has been conducting research and writing in the field of Islamic law, ethics and theology (Sunni and Shia) for more than two decades. In the last ten years, he has concentrated on social and political ethics, including interfaith and intrafaith relations, Islamic biomedical ethics and Islam and human rights. Dr. Sachedina's publications include *Islamic Messianism* (State University of New York, 1980); *Human Rights and the Conflicts of Culture*, co-authored (University of South Carolina, 1988); *The Just Ruler in Shiite Islam* (Oxford University Press, 1988); *The Prolegomena to the Qur'an* (Oxford University Press, 1998); *The Islamic Roots of Democratic Pluralism* (Oxford University Press, 2002); *Islamic Biomedical Ethics: Theory and Application* (Oxford University Press, February 2009); and *Islam and the Challenge of Human Rights*

(Oxford University Press, September 2009), in addition to numerous articles in academic journals. He is an American citizen born in Tanzania.

[2] Among modern scholars, the works of Taha Husayn, *al-Fitna al-Kubra* and *'Ali wa Banuh*, and 'Abbas Mahmud al-'Aqqad, *Abu al-Shuhada' Husayn ibn 'Ali,* mark a beginning in this direction of critical evaluation of early Islamic history. The important phase of "revisionism" is also marked by Abu al-Alā Mawdūdī's controversial (as far as Sunni Muslims are concerned) *Khilafat va Mulukiyyat*. This work has been refuted again and again by several Sunni authors who do not agree with al-Mawdūdī's objectivity in dealing with both 'Uthmān and Mu'āwiya's caliphates (see, for instance, Muhammad Ishaq's *Izhar-i Haqiqat bi Javab-i Khilafat va Mulukiyyat* and Mahmud Ahmad 'Abbasi's *Haqiqat-i Khilafat va Mulukiyyat*. Hamid Enayat, in *Modern Islamic Political Thought* (London, 1982, republished by Islamic Book Trust Kuala Lumpur), pages 181-194, reviews modern literature written on Imam Ḥusayn by Arab and Persian scholars. Unfortunately, Enayat did not read Urdu and was unable to take into account an important and rather controversial study by the learned scholar 'Ali Naqi Naqavi. *Shahid-i Insaniyyat* (1942), which precedes the Persian study of Ni'mat Allah Salihi Najafabadi, *Shahid-i Javid* (1968), based on the historical method.

CHAPTER ONE

Introduction

M.A. Rahman Sayeed Siddiqi

In the name of Allah,
the Compassionate, the Merciful.

In the ancient world, as in the modern world, instances of suppressing the truth are commonplace. The history of various nations provides ample evidence in this regard—a huge conflagration was lit by Nimrod for consigning Abraham to its flames on the charge of idol-breaking in the main temple of Babylon; Prophet Joseph had to accept imprisonment in Egypt for his chastity; Prophet Zecharia's body was sawed through for raising his voice against idol worship, which was openly practised in the kingdom of Judah; Jesus Christ was sentenced to be crucified by the Roman hierarchy for disseminating the Divine Message; history records a series of ordeals, persecutions and hostilities against preaching Islam by the Last Prophet, Muḥammad ﷺ.

The Karbala incident is assigned a prominent place among all historical events of selflessness, justice and sacrifice. The history of Karbala represents, on one hand, the tragic event, in so far as suppression of truthful people are concerned, and provides, on the other, a horrifying example of barbarism, in so far as atrocities of temporal authority is concerned.

While copious literature exists on the implications of Ḥusayn's martyrdom stressing mainly the spirit of his sacrifice and heroic deed, there is also a matter-of-fact approach to the Karbala issue by the so called rationalists who are at a loss to understand other than the worldly interest. Since no attempt has ever been made to examine the contest between Ḥusayn and Yazīd exclusively from the historical point of view, the rationalists ascribe these deductions in favour of Ḥusayn to blind faith. His departure from Medina is attributed to a campaign for power-seeking; his refusal to take the oath of allegiance to Yazīd is attributed to the formation of a political faction, and the Karbala battle is attributed to a clash of interest between two rival groups. As this unbalanced hostile criticism is likely to poison the view of the younger generation about Ḥusayn's sacrifice, it is essential to probe into the controversy in the light of historical records so that it becomes crystal clear that Ḥusayn's stand alone was justifiable. The main objections raised, in connection with the Karbala event, may be summarised as follows:

1. Why did Ḥusayn refuse to take the oath of allegiance in favour of Yazīd? Does not this refusal amount to a claim to his own right to caliphate?

2. If refusal to acknowledge the allegiance was a protest against hereditary right to caliphate, was not Ḥusayn's own claim to caliphate after 'Alī and Ḥasan tantamount to inheriting the caliphate for himself?

3. If Ḥusayn's ultimate aim was to reform Muslim society in the light of the Qur'an and *Sunnah*, was he not in a position to set right Yazīd's conduct without creating a rift in the community by refusing allegiance? His refusal created a barrier between him and Yazīd, which eventually resulted in the

bloody event of Karbala.

4. If a campaign against Yazīd was, according to Ḥusayn's point of view, a holy war in the cause of Allah why did Ḥusayn put forth the following three alternatives?

    a. Let him return to the place he had come from.

    b. Let him settle his case with Yazīd personally.

    c. Send him to the border area, where he would face what Muslims of that region are forced to face.

5. During that period, Muslim society had assumed an un-Islamic character. Rivalry among Arab tribes had reached its zenith. Had a person from the Umayyad tribe not come to the office of caliphate, would not the tribal enmity and disputes have constituted a danger to the Islamic state?

As all these issues have a direct bearing on the basic problem of caliphate, it would best to explain the concept of caliphate in a nutshell.

It should be borne in mind that the essence or spirit of political theory is the concept that the authority to make laws is not vested in anyone except Allah. No one is authorised to issue a command that others are obliged to obey.

> "*The command is for none but Allah; He has commanded that you worship none but Him. This is the right religion, but most people understand not.*" (Yūsuf 12:40)

It is, therefore, a logical conclusion that authority is vested solely in Almighty Allah. He alone is the lawmaker, and no human being, not even a prophet, is empowered to make a law.[1] The person who is appointed temporal authority, in accordance with the Islamic constitution, will, of course, be regarded as a vicegerent of the Supreme Being who will enforce only the delegated powers.

The advent of Islam with this chaste and pure doctrine was the most revolutionary force of the time. Due to its dynamic power a formidable community came into existence with the synthesis of sound and healthy elements. Further, being directly influenced by the living model of prophethood, which was an embodiment of unflinching righteousness and sublime character, the movement of Islam had combined in itself the power of both defending and assimilating the truth. Thus, the combination of these two forces actually constitutes "caliphate".

Every believer is Allah's vicegerent and, as such, Islam does not admit class division and economic or social distinction in its society. All individuals are treated on equal footing. Superiority is, of course, based on righteousness, personal capability and high moral character.

> "*Indeed, the noblest of you in Allah's sight is the best in conduct.*" (al-Ḥujurāt 49:13)

Caliphate is an elective office. But merely occupying the seat of caliphate does not prove that the occupant has a just right to this high office. One has to fulfil its intrinsic obligations and inherent duties. Prophet Muḥammad ﷺ never intended to lay the foundation of an empire purely from the material point of view. He strove hard to build a "*milla*" (community) which was fully equipped with high moral character, and to establish the kingdom of God with the help of self-purification, love and service to humanity. In view of these bare facts, only such a person deserves the office of caliphate who attains perfection from the moral point of view and is able to do full justice to the demands of leading humanity from the political point of view.

Let us first examine, in the light of historical

evidence, the genuineness of Yazīd's nomination as successor to his father Mu'āwiya. As a matter of fact, al-Mughīra ibn Shu'ba wanted to make the caliphate permanent in the Umayyad dynasty, obviously to ingratiate himself with Mu'āwiya. He suggested this point to Yazīd who, in turn, communicated it to Mu'āwiya. When the latter discussed the matter with al-Mughīra, he said, "You are well aware of differences and bloodshed among the Muslims since the time of 'Uthmān's martyrdom. I am, therefore, of opinion that Yazīd should be declared successor after obtaining votes of allegiance in his favour, so that, when you face the inevitable hour, he will be your successor on whom the Muslims may rely and there will not be any disturbance or bloodshed." On Mu'āwiya's query as to who would sponsor the mission, al-Mughīra replied that he would shoulder the responsibility of bringing round the Kufans, Ziyad should prepare the ground in Basra, and the responsibility of winning over the people of Ḥijaz may be assigned to Marwān ibn al-Ḥakam.[2]

At that time, Kufa and Basra were the political centres and Medina was regarded as the centre of savants and religious-minded people. All the matters of great import had to be referred to the elite of those places. Al-Mughīra, who was very influential in Kufa, sent a deputation consisting of prominent people of the city to wait on Mu'āwiya. The deputation visited Medina and mooted the proposal of nominating Yazīd as Mu'āwiya's successor. When Ziyad of Basra was asked to mobilise public opinion at his headquarters, he at once felt his own responsibility and exchanged views with his trustworthy chief 'Ubayd ibn Kawkab in the following terms: "This is an important issue pertaining to Islam attended with heavy responsibility. The careless temperament of Yazīd is now an open secret. You better apprise the Leader of the Believers of Yazīd's activities and advise him not to make haste in this matter."[3] 'Ubayd replied that it was not advisable to prejudice the Leader of the Believers against Yazīd. He would himself instruct Yazīd to give up his objectionable activities so that people might not find fault with him.

The situation in Ḥijaz was more complicated. Here lived a number of venerable personalities who could have presented themselves as qualified candidates for caliphate and hence there was every apprehension of the proposal being opposed. Marwān ibn al-Ḥakam was entrusted with the work of doing canvassing in Medina in favour of Yazīd. In this connection, Mu'āwiya addressed him tactfully in the following manner:

"I have grown old and am now exhausted.

> Nobody knows as to when the inevitable hour arrives. I am afraid that a rift may appear in the community after my death. I, therefore, deem it proper that my successor should be declared during my lifetime, in the best interest of the people. I require your advice in this regard. Put forth this proposal before the inhabitants of Medina and inform me of their reaction."[4]

The proposal was brought before the Medinans. Mu'āwiya had not nominated his successor in this letter. Since the proposal, in its general nature, appeared to be innocent, the audiences agreed to it. On being informed of this, Mu'āwiya was encouraged and nominated his son as his successor.

Marwān announced the nomination, which was met with severe opposition. 'Abd al-Rahman ibn Abī Bakr stood up and said to Marwān, "You and Mu'āwiya both utter a lie. This move is not meant for the welfare of the community. Caliphate is actually being converted into a Caesarian kingdom."

Marwān replied that the Leader of the Believers wanted to nominate Yazīd just like Abū Bakr and 'Umar had nominated their successors. To this, 'Abd al-Rahman retorted that the proposal was not in the way of Abū Bakr and 'Umar, but an exact replica of Caesar's policy. The two caliphs had never nominated their sons as successors. They even kept their relatives away from this high office. Marwan communicated all these details to Mu'āwiya. In the meantime, deputations from Medina and Basra reached Mu'āwiya's headquarters in Syria. Mu'āwiya, first, had a parley with a respectable representative of Medina named Muhammad ibn 'Amr ibn Hazm, who in the course of discussion remarked,

> "Every ruler is responsible before his subjects. You may think over twice about the person whom you intend to nominate as ruler."[5]

Later, Mu'āwiya asked for the opinion of al-Ahnaf ibn Qays, leader of the Basra deputation who was a statesman and belonged to the influential nobility of that city. He observed,

> "If we speak the truth, we are sure to offend you; if we utter a lie, there is an apprehension of being punished by God. You are aware of the day-to-day open and secret activities of Yazīd better than I am. In spite of this, if you consider him to be suitable for administering the affairs of the *ummah*, there is no need for any consultation. If this is not the case, do not get yourself involved in the affairs of this material world on the eve of your departure to the other

world. After all, we are compelled to comply with your orders."[6]

Despite such an opposition, Muʿāwiya was adamant on nominating Yazīd as his successor. Obtaining the consent of the people was just a formality. He won over some of the people with favour and clemency and some with threat and intimidation. As a result, the people of Iraq and Syria took the oath of allegiance. Ḥijaz was the main obstacle in the way, as it had been the centre of the descendants of the *Muhajirin* (migrants) and *Ansar* (helpers), the Prophet's ﷺ companions and their sons. As such Muʿāwiya undertook the journey to Medina and anticipated a danger, especially from five prominent people: ʿAbdullah ibn ʿUmar, ʿAbdullah ibn ʿAbbas, ʿAbdullah ibn Zubayr, Ḥusayn ibn ʿAlī and ʿAbd al-Rahman ibn Abi Bakr. Muʿāwiya met each of them separately and told them that all the people except themselves had accepted the proposal of Yazīd being his successor. ʿAbdullah ibn Zubayr was selected to represent on behalf of this group.

Enumerating the favours he had been showing to them, Muʿāwiya suggested that Yazīd would assume only the title of caliph, while the entire administration, appointment and dismissal of the administrative staff, collection of revenues and tributes and their expenditure would be controlled by them. In reply, ʻAbdullah ibn Zubayr said that there had been three precedents of electing the caliph.

First, the Prophet ﷺ did not nominate any one as his successor. He left the election of his successor to the free discretion of the people. Second, Abu Bakr nominated the best person from among the Prophet's ﷺ Companions with whom he had no family connections. Third, ʻUmar left to the advisory council, election of one of the people mentioned in the panel of six names. Barring these, no fourth proposal would be acceptable. When Muʻāwiya found that the group of these five people would not come round easily, he held out a threat that in case they opposed the proposal, he would resort to force.

Subsequently, he came out and announced to the waiting public that the prominent men of Mecca had taken oath of allegiance and that others should also follow suit. After Muʻāwiya's return, though the truth dawned on the people, nobody had the courage to protest against him. During the days of Muʻāwiya's death illness, when Yazīd was away from Damascus, the former prepared a will for Yazīd, alerting him against the impending dangers so that he can smoothly run the administration. The text of the will is as follows:

> "My dear son, I have paved the way for you, removing all the hurdles. All the antagonists have been defeated and they are made to kneel down before you. Moreover, a big treasury has been raised. The crux of the problem facing you is the administration of caliphate. In this field, none is your rival except Ḥusayn ibn 'Alī, 'Abdullah ibn 'Umar, 'Abd al-Rahman ibn Abi Bakr and 'Abdullah ibn Zubayr. 'Abdullah ibn 'Umar is a harmless person. He is not concerned with anything except worship of God. 'Abd al-Rahman ibn Abi Bakr lacks courage and bravery. He follows the path of his fellow beings. Ḥusayn ibn 'Alī will, of course, prove a danger. The people of Iraq will surely bring him against you. If this happens and Ḥusayn is brought under your control, forgive him, as he is closely related to the Prophet and he has a right to the caliphate. But the person who adopts deceptive methods like a fox and attacks like a tiger is 'Abdullah ibn Zubayr. If he comes to terms, that is well and good, otherwise he should not be spared. The moment you catch hold of him, cut him into pieces."[7]

This is the story of the fake process adopted to bring Yazīd to the office of the caliphate. Let us now examine the implications of Ḥusayn's refusal to take the oath of fealty in favour of Yazīd.

1. After the death of Mu'āwiya, when Walid, governor of Medina, demanded the oath from Ḥusayn, at the instance of Yazīd, Ḥusayn replied, "A man of my position cannot take the oath of allegiance secretly. When the general public will be called on to take the oath, I shall also be among them."

   Ḥusayn's reply is self-explanatory. It lays emphasis on the point that Yazīd was not elected by the people by their free will. Had the authoritative power not been employed in favour of Yazīd and had an election been held on correct lines, Yazīd would have never ascended the throne of caliphate in the presence of capable personalities like Ḥusayn and 'Abdullah ibn Zubayr.

2. No doubt, Ḥusayn had a claim for caliphate, but it did not mean that he intended to seize power in opposition to the general opinion. Had Ḥusayn been elected mainly on his personal merit by majority of votes, his succession to caliphate would have never been reckoned as hereditary.

3. From the very beginning, Yazīd's idiosyncrasy was conducive to coercion and cruelty. The

autocratic traditions that came into vogue during Mu'āwiya's period had made the confusion worse. As a result, Yazīd did not hesitate in adopting the lawful and unlawful, fair or foul means in the safeguard of his own interest. The governors, advisers, high-ranking officials and people belonging to the higher strata of society were hankering after personal ends. Ḥusayn's non-cooperation with Mu'āwiya was in itself a gesture on his part that he stood to resist the undesirable change. The march of events had taken an ugly turn under the aegis of the ruling class. When the ideal in its pristine purity determined by Islam was lost, there remained only the idols of selfishness, lust for worldly power, pomp and pageantry. Ḥusayn was not prepared to make any compromise with an un-Islamic proposition of electing a caliph. Thus, there were two distinct ideologies that stood poles apart, creating a rift, but at the same time showing demarcation between truth and falsehood.

4. Refusal to take the oath of allegiance in Yazīd's favour was a challenge for the opposition. In view of the message communicated by the Kufans inviting Ḥusayn to come over to Kufa,

he became optimistic that footing would be secured to defend the sacred legacy of Islam left by his grandfather, the Last Prophet ﷺ. He, therefore, undertook the journey to Kufa despite strong opposition by his relatives, friends, well-wishers and sympathisers. On his way to Kufa, when he received the tragic news of his cousin, Muslim ibn ʻAqil's murder at the hands of the governor of Kufa, the astounding information of the Kufans' betrayal and ultimately saw that there was none to cooperate with him, he suggested the aforementioned three alternatives obviously to gain time and power for the defence of truth in the future. When the autocratic regime, operated according to its own whims and fancies, ignoring the cannons of the relevant Islamic law, no recourse was left for Ḥusayn except to defend the truth at the cost of his life.

5. The contention that tribal enmity and disputes would have taken place if Yazīd had not assumed the office of caliphate is not justifiable. All that can be said in reply to this question is that the recognised Islamic tenets cannot be sacrificed at the altar of the diplomatic expediency. Islam does not preach

to change colours according to the dictates of time. It insists on enforcing divine law in the face of all eventualities. Moreover, Islam is not the product of time, nor does it depend on the issues taking their birth as a result of the change of the ruling dynasties. Its principles are universal and immutable. It cannot make a compromise with ever-changing tendencies and innovations. Its main object is to give a lead in all times and to struggle against falsehood.

Notes

[1] From an Islamic point of view, although the Prophet is not a lawmaker, in his personal capacity, he formulates by-laws in the light of divine law. This is the reason why the Prophet's traditions are unanimously regarded as one of the sources of Islamic law next to the Holy Qur'an.

[2] *Tarikh-e Islam*, Part II (Darul Musannefin, Azamgarh), p. 24, with reference to *Khilafat o Mulukiyyat* by Maulana Abu al-A'la al-Mawdudi.

[3] *Tarikh-e Islam*, pp. 25-26.

[4] *Tarikh-e Islam*, vol. II, p. 25.

[5] *Tarikh-e Islam*, part II.

[6] *Khilafat o Mulukiyyat.*

[7] *Tarikh-e Islam*, vol. II, p. 29.

در معنئ حرّیتِ اسلامیہ و سرِّ حادثۂ کربلا

ہر کہ پیمان با ھو الموجود بست / گردنش از بندِ ہر معبود رست
مومن از عشق است و عشق از مومن است / عشق را ناممکنِ ما ممکن است
عقل سفّاک است و اُو سفّاک تر / پاک تر، چالاک تر، بیباک تر
عقل در پیچاکِ اسباب و علل / عشق چوگان بازِ میدانِ عملؒ
عشق صید از زورِ بازو افگند / عقل مکّار است و دامے می زند
عقل را سرمایہ از بیم و شک است / عشق را عزم و یقین لاینفک است
آن کند تعمیر تا ویران کند / این کند ویران کہ آباد ان کند
عقل چون باد است ارزان در جہان / عشق کمیاب و بہائے اُو گران
عقل محکم از اساسِ چون و چند / عشق عُریان از لباسِ چون و چند
عقل میگوید کہ خود را پیش کن / عشق گوید امتحانِ خویش کن
عقل با غیر آشنا از اکتساب / عشق از فضل است و با خود در حساب
عقل گوید شاد شو آباد شو / عشق گوید بندہ شو آزاد شو
عشق را آرامِ جان حُرّیت است / ناقہ اش را ساربان حُرّیت است

آن شنیدستی کہ ہنگامِ نبرد / عشق با عقلِ ہوس پرور چہ کرد
آن امامِ عاشقان پُورِ بتولؓ / سروِ آزادے زِ بُستانِ رسولؐ
اللہ اللہ بائے بسم اللہ پدر / معنئ ذبحِ عظیم آمد پسر
بہرِ آن شہزادۂ خیر الملل / دوشِ ختم المرسلین نعم الجمل
سُرخ رُو عشقِ غیور از خوُنِ اُوؐ / شوخئ این مصرع از مضمونِ اُو

در میانِ اُمّت آن کیوان جناب
همچو حرفِ قُل هُو اللہ در کتاب

موسیٰ و فرعون و شبیرؑ و یزید
این دو قوت از حیات آید پدید

زندہ حق از قوتِ شبیریؑ است
باطل آخر داغِ حسرت میری است

چُون خلافت رشتہ از قرآن گسیخت
حُرّیت را زهر اندر کام ریخت

خاست آن سر جلوۂ خیرالاُمَمؐ
چون سحابِ قبلہ باران در قدم

بر زمینِ کربلا بارید و رفت
لالہ در ویرانہ ہا کارید و رفت

تا قیامت قطعِ استبداد کرد
موجِ خونِ اُو چمن ایجاد کرد

بہرِ حق در خاک و خون غلطیدہ است
پس بنائے لا الٰہ گردیدہ است

مدعایش سلطنت بودے اگر
خود نکردے با چُنین سامان سفر

دُشمناں چُوں ریگِ صحرا لاتعد
دوستانِ اُو بہ یزدان ہم عدد

سرِّ ابراہیمؑ و اسماعیلؑ بود
یعنی آن اجمال را تفصیل بود

عزمِ اُو چُون کوہساران اُستوار
پائیدار و تند سیر و کامگار

تیغ بہرِ عزّتِ دین است و بس
مقصدِ اُو حفظِ آئین است و بس

ماسوااللہ را مسلمان بندہ نیست
پیشِ فرعونے سَرش افگندہ نیست

خُونِ اُو تفسیرِ این اسرار کرد
ملّتِ خوابیدہ را بیدار کرد

تیغِ لا چُون از میان بیرون کشید
از رگِ اربابِ باطل خُون کشید

نقشِ اِلّا اللہ بر صحرا نوشت
سطرِ عُنوانِ نجاتِ ما نوشت

رمزِ قرآن از حُسینؑ آموختیم
ز آتشِ اُو شعلہ ہا اندوختیم

شوکتِ شام و فرِ بغداد رفت
سطوتِ غرناطہ ہم از یاد رفت

تارِ ما از زخمہ اش لرزان ہنوز!
تازہ از تکبیرِ اُو ایمان ہنوز!

اے صبا اے پیکِ دُور افتادگان
اشکِ ما بر خاکِ پاکِ اُو رسان

CHAPTER TWO

The Significance of Islamic Freedom and the Secret of the Karbala Event

Muhammad Iqbal,
Poet of the East

1. Whoever makes a covenant with the Omnipresent,
   Is freed from the bondage of all (false) gods.

2. A believer's existence is dependent on Love,
   While Love for its manifestation is dependent on the believer.
   What is impossible for mortals is rendered possible through (the dynamic force of) Love.

3. Reason is ruthlessly sharp, but Love is sharper;

It is chaster, more shrewd, more daring.

4. Reason is lost in the maze of cause and effect;
   Love is the champion in the field of action.

5. Love captures its prey through sheer strength,
   While Reason captures through deceit by laying a snare.

6. Doubt and fear are the assets of Reason;
   Self-Confidence and firmness of purpose are the integral parts of love.

7. Reason builds to destroy,
   While Love destroys to re-create.

8. Reason has a little value like the air in this world;
   Love is highly inestimable.

9. Reason is absorbed in questions of how and how much;
   Love, in its purity, transcends them.

10. Reason advises self-assertion,
    While Love counsels self-examination.

11. Reason is indebted to other things for knowledge;
    Love originates in grace (of God) and is contended with self-knowledge.

12. Reason says, "Be happy and prosper",
    While Love advises, "Surrender thyself and be free."

13. Love finds both comfort and consolation in freedom;
    Freedom is its source of guidance.

14. Have you not heard how summarily, on the occasion of the great conflict,[1]
    Love dealt with conceited Reason.

15. That Imam of all lovers, the son of Fatima,[2]
    That cypress in the Prophet's garden.

16. What a marvellous phenomenon!
    (Ḥusayn's) great grandfather (Ishmael) set the first example of self-sacrifice,[3]
    Whose meaning and significance became fully explicit in him (Ḥusayn), the great grandson.[4]

17. For that Prince of ideal character (Ḥusayn),
    The Last Prophet offered his own shoulder as a substitute for a camel's back.[5]

18. Love's majestic visage glowing with pride because of the blood of the martyred Ḥusayn.
    The colourfulness of this line is due to the theme of martyrdom.

19. Ḥusayn's unique position in the Muslim *ummah*,
    Is like the honoured place occupied by the *surah* (al-Ikhlāṣ) in the Qur'an.[6]

20. Moses and Pharoah, Ḥusayn and Yazīd—

They are but the conflicting forces of life.

21. Truth survives and triumphs because of Ḥusayn.
Falsehood is destined to meet with failure and grief.

22. The moment the leadership of the faithful broke the link with the Qur'an,
Human freedom was poisoned in the blood.

23. There arose a man, the best of the best among nations,
Like a rain-laden eastern cloud, bringing water to a parched, rocky soil.

24. This cloud rained for a moment on Karbala,
Causing the desert to bloom and passed on.

25. He (Ḥusayn) exterminated tyranny forever;
From his martyred blood there rose a new garden (of human values) in the wilderness.

26. Writhing in dust and blood for defending truth,
He became the cornerstone of *La Ilaha Illallah* (There is no god except Allah).[7]

27. Had power been his objective,
He would not have set forth so ill equipped.

28. His enemies were in multitude just like the sands of the desert,
While the number of his companions was equal

to the numerical value of the word *Yazdan* (*i.e.* only seventy-two).[8]

29. In him (Ḥusayn), the mystery Abraham and Ishmael unfolds and expounds itself.
    He is the illustration of their faith.

30. His will was firm as a rock,
    Swift and triumphant (like a river).

31. The sword was for him a weapon meant solely for the defence of the faith
    And the protection of divine law.

32. The Muslim owes allegiance to none but Allah.
    His head never bows before a tyrant.

33. This was the secret that Ḥusayn unveiled with his blood
    And roused his people from slumber.

34. When he (Ḥusayn) unsheathed the sword of denial of false gods,
    He caused the blood to flow from the veins of their supporters.[9]

35. He inscribed the words *illallah* (except Allah) on the desert sands of Karbala.[10]
    Thus, he imprinted the first line of the charter of our salvation.

36. It is from Ḥusayn that we have learnt the hidden meaning or the Holy Word (Qur'an).
The flames of burning faith we borrowed from his fire.

37. The splendour that was once Syria and Baghdad,
And the glory of Granada, are all now a forgotten tale.

38. At the touch of Ḥusayn's plectrum the strings of our being still vibrate;
His cry of *Allahu Akbar* still keeps our faith alive.

39. O Wind, thou messenger of far-flung people,
Present our tears to the sacred dust that covers Ḥusayn's remains.

Notes

[1] It refers to the battle of Karbala, which was fought between Ḥusayn and Yazīd on the former's refusal to take the oath of allegiance in favour of Yazīd, because Yazīd's nomination to caliphate was contrary to the basic principles of Islamic democracy.

[2] This couplet refers to a *ḥadīth* of the Prophet in which he characterises his two grandsons (Ḥasan and Ḥusayn) as chiefs of the youths of Paradise.

[3] The allusion pertains to Ishmael, the son of Abraham, who, at the divine instance, in a dream, resolved to sacrifice the life of Ishmael by slaughtering him. When

Abraham was about to commit this act, Allah saved Ishmael's life and accepted the sacrifice of a sheep in his place. This is described in the Qur'an as the Great Sacrifice.

[4] Ḥusayn was born in the lineage of Ishmael. He was killed in Karbala in a struggle to defend the basic values of Islam. Dr. Iqbal says that the significance of the "Great Sacrifice" is practically manifested in Ḥusayn's martyrdom.

[5] The couplet refers to the most familiar anecdote that once, on the occasion of *Id al-Fitr*, Ḥasan and Ḥusayn insisted on having a camel to go to the mosque for Id prayer as some of the Arab elite did on that day. The Prophet had no camel, so he pacified his grandsons by seating them on his two shoulders in place of a camel, and taking them to the prayer.

[6] According to a *ḥadīth*, *surah* 112 (al-Ikhlāṣ) occupies a prominent place in the Holy Qur'an, and that whoever recites this *surah* is regarded to have recited the whole Qur'an.

[7] The couplet refers to the well-known quatrain supposed to have been composed by the famous Saint Khoja Moinuddin Chishti of Ajmer. He says that Ḥusayn revolted against the false demand of Yazīd and never took the oath of allegiance although he had to sacrifice his life in the battle for defending the truth. Ḥusayn is the torch-bearer of the message underlying the article of faith.

[8] Ḥusayn had only seventy-two followers with him. This number is equal to the numerical value of the word *Yazdan*.

[9] The "sword of denial" construes the proclamation of Allah's sovereignty and total negation of one man's

subjugation to the other.

[10] Faith in the sovereignty of Allah alone brings salvation to man on the Day of Judgment.

CHAPTER THREE

The History of Karbala

Abul Kalam Azad

It is a commonplace that the fame enjoyed by a person is seldom in proportion to his real greatness. Strange as it may seem, the personages who reach the highest pitch of grandeur, sanctity and fame are associated with legends rather than historical facts. In view of this experience, Ibn Khaldun, pioneer philosophical historian, laid down a general principle that the more an incident becomes popular, the more a network of unfounded tales and stories is woven around it. The German poet Goethe states the same truth in a different way. He says that when human greatness reaches its peak, it becomes a legend.

The important place Ḥusayn occupies in Islamic history is too well known and requires no elucidation. Subsequent to the period of the Prophet's ﷺ true successors, the incident that had a powerful impact on the religious and political history of Islam is the tragic event of Ḥusayn's martyrdom. It may not be an exaggeration to say that no tragic incident that has occurred in this world caused humanity to shed tears so profusely as this particular event. More than 1,300 years have passed since this soul-stirring event in Islamic history and still the month of Muharram brings to the mind of every Muslim a vivid remembrance of the noble sacrifice offered by Ḥusayn.

In spite of this, how curious it is that a powerful and tragic event of great import has assumed the shape more of a fable than a historical fact. If a fact finder wishes to study this event in the light of reliable evidences of history, in most of the cases he will be disappointed. The existing popular material on the subject is meant only for narration in religious assemblies, exciting the feelings of sorrow and grief for the martyrs.

A few details of the event leading to the martyrdom of Ḥusayn are given here. It should be borne in mind that this description does not seek to make a historical criticism but aims at presenting bare facts relating to Ḥusayn's martyrdom in chronological order.

Cause of Differences Between Ḥusayn and Yazīd

Ahl al-Bayt, members of the Prophet's ﷺ family, had a valid claim to the caliphate for themselves. Soon after the death of Mu'āwiya ibn Abī Sufyān, his son Yazīd declared himself the caliph since he had been nominated a successor to Mu'āwiya during his lifetime. Yazīd demanded allegiance from Ḥusayn ibn 'Alī. As the nomination to caliphate was contrary to the spirit of the Islamic constitution, Ḥusayn ibn 'Alī was averse to it and he, therefore, refused to take the oath of allegiance in favour of Yazīd.

Ḥusayn's Journey to Kufa

Ḥusayn undertook a journey to Kufa, as he was invited to that place by the Kufans with a message that conditions obtaining in Kufa were propitious for Ḥusayn's caliphate. In the course of the journey, he happened to meet at al-Sifah the well-known poet al-Farazdaq, who composed panegyrics on the *Ahl al-Bayt*. When interrogated by Ḥusayn about the people of Kufa, the poet answered,

"At heart they are with you, but they would raise their swords against you." Ḥusayn confirmed this answer and said, "Now the matter is left to Allah. His will, will be done. His commandments are issued every moment. If His will is in consonance with ours, we praise Him. If our hopes are frustrated, we still can bear the reward of patience and resignation."

Arrival of Al-Hurr Ibn Yazīd

Ḥusayn's party had advanced only a little distance beyond al-Qadisiyya when al-Hurr ibn Yazīd appeared with a force of a thousand armed men and followed him and his men intending to keep a close watch on them till they came face to face with 'Ubaydullah ibn Ziyad, governor of Iraq, and his men. After the midday and afternoon prayers, Ḥusayn addressed his companions as well as the force headed by al-Hurr:

"You will please God if you adhere to righteousness and support the claim of the right person. We the members of the Prophet's ﷺ family have a stronger claim to caliphate than others. They rule over you tyrannically. If you dislike us and do not concede our right, if you have gone back on the promises contained in

> your communications addressed to me and conveyed through messengers, I am willingly prepared to go back."

Advancing further, at a place known as al-Bayda, Ḥusayn again addressed those present in the following words:

> "O people, the Prophet said that whoever comes across a ruler who perpetrates cruelty and transgresses the divine limits breaks the covenant made with Allah, violates the Prophet's traditions and rules over the people with coercion. If he does not oppose that ruler with word and deed, Allah will not allot him a good abode in the life hereafter. Look, they have become the devil's followers and are opposed to Allah's commandments. Corruption has appeared. They are violating the limits imposed by Allah. They are in illegal possession of booty. The lawful is made unlawful and the unlawful is rendered lawful. I am the right person to prevent them from going astray and lead them to truth and justice. Your numerous letters were received and messengers approached me with the message of allegiance. You have pledged your word that you would not betray me, nor would you hand me over to my enemies. If you abide by your

pledge, you will be on the right paths. However, it is not beyond our expectation if you breach the promise. You have meted out a similar treatment to my cousin. Whoever trusts you is actually under the spell of illusion. Beware, you have already harmed yourself, and even now you continue to harm yourself. You have lost your share and marred your fortune. Whoever breaks the promise will break it to the detriment of his own self. It may be that Allah will soon rescue me from your hands."

At another place, he observed:

"You witness the existing state of affairs. The world has changed its colours. It is completely devoid of virtue. Only the sediment is left. Alas, do you not see that truth has been relegated to the backstage. Falsehood is deliberately being acted on. There is no one to prevent wrongdoing. It is high time a believer tried to defend the truth for the sake of Allah. I wish to die a martyr's death. It is an offence, in itself, to live with oppressors."[1]

Listening to this address, someone named Zuhayr among the audience stood up and spoke as follows:

"O son of the Prophet, may Allah be with you.

> We have listened to your discourse. By God, if the world were eternal and we were to live therein forever, even then we would be prepared to give up our lives for extending assistance to you. We would like to die with you rather than lead an eternal life."

Retort to Al-Hurr's Threat

In the course of the journey, al-Hurr had been repeatedly threatening Ḥusayn that if he waged war, he would surely be killed. Once roused to indignation, Ḥusayn replied, "Do you frighten me with death? Has cruelty gone to that extreme that you people intend to kill me? I am at a loss to understand in what terms I will reply to you. I want to repeat the same words uttered by one of the Prophet's ﷺ companions while proceeding on a *jihād* expedition in reply to a threat by his brother: "I am proceeding. Death does not mean humiliation for a brave person when his intention is genuine and performs *jihād* in the cause of Islam."[2]

Kufans Arrive

At a place known as 'Udhayb al-Hijanat, four horsemen were seen coming from Kufa. Ḥusayn asked them about the situation in the city. They replied that at the time of their departure, the citizens were being persuaded through bribery. At heart they were for Ḥusayn, but they would draw their swords against him.

Al-Tirimmah Ibn 'Adi's Offer

At this juncture, one of Ḥusayn's well-wishers, al-Tirimmah ibn 'Adi said, "By God, I am making a keen observation, but I see nobody who may stand by your side. Death seems to be inevitable for you, if the people who are following rush on you. I never saw anywhere as big a crowd as witnessed behind Kufa. They all have assembled to fight against one individual—Ḥusayn. I advise you not to move an inch further; if you want to go to a place where you would be quite immune from enemies, you may follow me. I shall take you to my mountain, Aja'. Within a period of less than ten days,, you will find 20,000 strong men belonging to the Tay' tribe arrayed before you armed with swords. As long as they are vigilant, nobody will have the courage to look at you with an evil intent."

Ḥusayn invoked Allah's blessings on him for his "offer" and said that he had a commitment with the men following him and, in view of this, he could not go a step forward. He said, "Nobody can predict how the dispute between us and our enemies will end."[3]

Ibn Ziyad's Letter

The next day, Ḥusayn rode on horseback and posted his men at strategic points for defence. Al-Hurr took exception to it. A tussle continued between the two for a long time. Eventually, an armed rider was seen coming from Kufa. He presented a communication addressed to al-Hurr by Ibn Ziyad, governor of Kufa, which read as follows:

> "I do not allow Ḥusayn to stay at any place. He should not be permitted to get down anywhere except in an open space. See that he does not take refuge either in a fort or a fertile piece of land. My messenger will remain with you to see how far you comply with my order."

Al-Hurr informed Ḥusayn of the contents of the governor's letter and told him that he was helpless. As such, he could only allow him to encamp in an open place in a desert.

Zuhayr suggested that a fight with the force that existed at that time was far easier than with the massive army that was expected to arrive later.

Ḥusayn disagreed, because he did not like to

initiate war.[4]

Eventually, on 2 Muharram 61 AH, Ḥusayn with his entourage camped at a forlorn place known as Karbala, situated at a long distance from the Euphrates with a hill in between the two.[5]

'Umar Ibn Sa'd's Arrival

The next day, 'Umar ibn Sa'd ibn Abi Waqqas arrived with an army of 4,000 Kufans. 'Ubaydullah ibn Ziyad deputed him on this expedition by force. 'Umar never wanted the situation to take a serious turn. He tried to settle the matter amicably. No sooner did he arrive at Karbala than he sent a messenger to Ḥusayn inquiring the reason of his arrival. In reply, Ḥusayn stated that the Kufans had invited him. He further added that in case they disliked his arrival, he was prepared to go back.

Ibn Ziyad's Stern Attitude

'Umar ibn Sa'd was delighted by this reply and became optimistic. He addressed a letter to 'Ubaydullah ibn Ziyad explaining the position. In reply, he issued the following instructions:

> "Ask Ḥusayn first to pledge allegiance to Yazīd with all his followers, and then we will see what

should be done. See that water is not supplied to Ḥusayn and his companions. They should not have even a drop of water, just as 'Uthmān ibn 'Affan was deprived of it."

Friction on Water

Being constrained by 'Ubaydullah's order, 'Umar ibn Sa'd posted 500 infantrymen to guard the river bank. The water supply to Ḥusayn and his party was cut off. As such, Ḥusayn ordered his brother al-'Abbas ibn 'Alī to fetch water from the river with thirty horsemen and twenty infantrymen. Arriving at the bank, they were resisted by the guard commander 'Amr ibn al-Ḥajjāj. A regular struggle ensued. Eventually, al-'Abbas succeeded in getting twenty leather bags filled with water.

Ḥusayn Meets 'Umar Ibn Sa'd

In the evening, Ḥusayn sent a messenger to 'Umar ibn Sa'd for a parley in the night. They both set off from their respective tents, each followed by 20 horsemen and met midway. They had a talk in private till late in the night. Although the talk was quite confidential, the lobby circle revealed that Ḥusayn suggested to 'Umar that they should leave their armies at Karbala and both go to Yazīd. 'Umar replied that if he acted according to this suggestion, his house would be destroyed. To this, Ḥusayn replied that he would have it reconstructed. 'Umar said that his entire property would be confiscated. Ḥusayn guaranteed that he would compensate from his own property situated in Ḥijaz. But 'Umar never agreed to it.[6] Subsequently, they had three more interviews with each other.

Ḥusayn's Three Conditions

Ḥusayn offered three alternatives:

1. Let him go back to the place he had come from.
2. Let him have his case decided by Yazīd himself.
3. Let him go to a border place.

After protracted negotiations, 'Umar ibn Sa'd wrote to Ibn Ziyad again as follows:

> "Allah has extinguished the fire of mischief. He has resolved the differences and created unity. He had set right the community's case. Ḥusayn held out a promise to accept any of the three alternatives. Therein lies yours as well as the community's welfare."

Shimr's Opposition

The letter created a favourable reaction on Ibn Ziyad. He appreciated Umar's efforts and said that the proposal was acceptable. Opposing the proposal, Shimr ibn Dhi al-Jawshan said,

> "Ḥusayn is now in our grip. If he escapes without taking the oath of allegiance, he might gain respect and power and, comparatively, you may be rendered weak and helpless. It is advisable that he be kept under watch until he surrenders himself. I am told that Ḥusayn and 'Umar hold secret talks at night."

Ibn Ziyad's Reply

This advice was approved and Shimr was deputed with a letter containing the following:

> "If Ḥusayn surrenders himself with all his companions, there should be no war and he should be sent to me alive. If he does not agree, there is no other alternative except war. Shimr has been instructed that as long as 'Umar complies with my orders, the former should obey him, otherwise he should remove 'Umar and take over the command of the army. Ḥusayn should be murdered and his head be

sent over to me."

In this letter, 'Umar was severely admonished with a warning that he was not deputed to defend Ḥusayn and offer him advice. Further, the letter contained the following specific instructions:

> "My orders are clear. If he surrenders himself, he should be sent to me alive. If he refuses, he should be attacked unhesitatingly. Shed his blood and disfigure his body, as he deserves it. After killing him, have his body trampled by horses, because he is a rebel and has deserted the community. I have resolved that if he is murdered, all these will be done. If you obey my orders, you will be eligible for a reward, and if you contravene them, you will be dismissed."[7]

Shimr handed over this letter to 'Umar ibn Sa'd, who reluctantly agreed to comply with the orders.

The Army's Preliminary Movement

After the evening prayer, 'Umar ibn Sa'd ordered his army to move. From the opposite side, al-'Abbas appeared with twenty horsemen. 'Umar informed him of the reply he received from 'Ubaydullah ibn Ziyad, which was conveyed to Ḥusayn.

Exchange of Words Between Men of Rival Forces

In the meantime, there was an exchange of dialogues between the representatives of the rival parties. From Ḥusayn's side, Habib ibn Mazahir came forward and said, "The worst people in Allah's eyes are those who present themselves before Him with hands stained with the blood of the Prophet's ﷺ descendants and of the pious people of Kufa."

'Urwa ibn Qays, from the opposite side, replied, "Boast as much as you can. Carry on propaganda about your own piety and purification."

To this Zahīr said, "Allah Himself has purified these people and led them to the right path. Fear God and do not be an accomplice to the wrongdoers by killing godly people."

When Ḥusayn came to know about the contents of Ibn Ziyad's letter, he said that confrontation might be avoided on that day, so they might be able to pray to God and ask for His forgiveness. He added, "God knows how much I am fond of Allah's worship and reciting verses from His Book." This message being conveyed, the hostile army retreated.[8]

During the night, Ḥusayn told his followers that the enemy was interested in him alone. After taking his life, the enemy would not bother about others.

Hence, he advised his companions to disperse along with his family members. The relatives of Muslim ibn 'Aqil were advised to go back, as Muslim's murder was too big a sacrifice.

They unanimously replied, "If we disperse, people will accuse us that we deserted our sheikh, leader and cousin. They will criticise us for never throwing an arrow, never using a spear and never wielding a sword. Never! We will never do that. We would sacrifice our property, life and progeny. We will fight along with you. We shall meet the same fate as yours. Allah may not keep us alive after you leave the world."

Ḥusayn's other companions also stood up and emphatically assured him of their cooperation at the risk of their lives.[9]

From the march of events, Ḥusayn's ailing son Zayn al-'Abidin came to the conclusion that the calamity was inevitable. When Ḥusayn's sister Zaynab came to know about it, she started shrieking and crying. Ḥusayn tried to pacify her, exhorting her, "What is all this, sister? I am afraid our faith and endurance are overpowered by our passions and devilish forces." Zaynab replied that she could not control herself when Ḥusayn was killing himself with his own hands. Ḥusayn answered that such was

Allah's will. This reply added much to Zaynab's distress, and she went out of control due to excessive grief. Witnessing this, Ḥusayn made a lengthy speech on patience and perseverance. He observed:

> "Sister, I fear Allah. Take solace from Allah's mercy. Death is destined for each and every living being. Even those living in Heaven cannot lead an eternal life. When everything is mortal in this world, why is there so much distress and grief at the thought of death? For every Muslim, the Prophet's life provides a model. What does this model teach us? It teaches us to have forbearance and perseverance. It also teaches us to rely on Allah and to resign ourselves to Allah's will. We should not deviate from that teaching."[10]

Ḥusayn and his companions spent the whole night offering prayer, invoking Allah's forgiveness, weeping and crying. A division of the enemy's cavalry had been patrolling round Ḥusayn's camp.

10 Muharram: War Begins

On 10 Muharram, Friday, 'Umar ibn Sa'd set out with his army. Ḥusayn too posted his men at strategic points. Altogether, his army consisted of only seventy-two men—thirty-two horsemen and forty infantrymen. The flag was held by Ḥusayn's brother al-'Abbas ibn 'Alī. Behind the camp, a trench was dug, which was filled with fire. Shimr who went past the camp on a galloping horse noticed the fire and cried aloud, "Ḥusayn, did you accept fire before the Day of Resurrection?" Ḥusayn retorted, "O son of a Shepherd, you deserve fire more than anyone else."

One of Ḥusayn's men, Muslim ibn 'Awsaja sought permission to shoot an arrow at him, as he was standing at point-blank range. Ḥusayn refused, as he did not want to initiate war.[11]

Ḥusayn's Discourse to the Enemy

As the enemy forces advanced, Ḥusayn raised his hands, praying to God. When the enemy approached, he mounted a camel, kept the Qur'an in front and addressed the enemy forces as follows:

> "O people, listen to me. Do not be rash. Let me admonish you. Let me say a few words in my justification and let me explain the reason for my arrival here. If my excuse is reasonable and if you can accept it, do justice in my case. You would be lucky and desist from taking arms against me. Even after hearing me, if you refuse to accept the excuse, I will be ready for you.

Rush on me all at once. Do not allow me a moment's respite. Whatever the eventual outcome, I place confidence in God, who supports the righteous.

"O people, remember my lineage. Pause to think for a while who I am. Take stock of your conscience! Is it fair for you to kill me and discard the respect due to me? Am I not the son of your Prophet's daughter and the son of his cousin? Is the leader of martyrs Ḥamza not my father's uncle? Is Ja'far at al-Tayyar not my uncle? Do you not remember the Prophet's famous words 'the chiefs of Paradise's youths' in reference to me and my brother? If my statement is true—and it is certainly true, because since the time I was conscious of myself, I have not uttered a lie—then tell me, is it right for you to receive me with unsheathed swords? If you do not believe in my word, there are people among you who can testify to the correctness of my statement. They can tell you whether they heard the Prophet's words about me and my brother. Should this fact not prevent you from shedding my blood? By God, the Prophet has no son on the earth's surface except me. I am the direct descendant and grandson of your Prophet. Do you want to kill me because I have taken someone's life? Did I shed anyone's blood? Have I usurped anyone's wealth? Tell me, what is the matter? What is my fault?"

Ḥusayn repeatedly asked this question, but nobody answered. At last, he called out by name Kufa's prominent people and inquired whether they had not written to him, "The fruits are ripe, the soil has become green and the canals are overflowing. If you come, you will come to the great army of your own. Come soon."

A Kufan's Reply

With that, those people opened their mouths and said they had never written anything to that effect. Ḥusayn expressed surprise at this and cried out, "What a blatant lie!" Ḥusayn again called out loudly, "O people, since you dislike me, it is better that I be released and go back."

At this juncture, one of the Kufans said, "Is it not advisable for you to surrender yourself to your cousins? They will mete out the treatment befitting your position. You will not be harmed by them."

Humiliation Unacceptable

To this, Ḥusayn answered, "All of you are tarred with the same brush. O man, do you want Banu Hashim to demand ransom for one more life, in addition to that of Muslim ibn 'Aqil? No, I will not surrender myself to them in humiliation."[12]

Al-Hurr Joins Ḥusayn's Army

When Ibn Sa'd ordered his army to advance, al-Hurr asked him whether he really wanted to fight against Ḥusayn? Ibn Sa'd replied, "Yes a battle would be fought in which heads will be cut and hands will be amputated from shoulders." Listening to this, al-Hurr left his own place and proceeded slowly towards Ḥusayn's camp. One of his tribe's men, Muhajir ibn Aws, asked whether he wanted to attack Ḥusayn. Al-Hurr kept quiet. Suspecting him due to his reticence, Muhajir said, "I never found you in such a state during any war. If I am asked to name the bravest man in Kufa, I can point out none except you. But what are you doing now?"

Al-Hurr grew serious and replied, "By God, I am making a choice between Hell and Heaven. And by God, I have selected Heaven, even if I am cut to pieces." With those words, he whipped his horse and joined Ḥusayn's army. He presented himself before

Ḥusayn and said, "O son of the Prophet, I am the same unfortunate person who prevented you from going back. I pursued you all along the way and compelled you to encamp at this place. I never suspected that these people would not concede your terms and would go to such extremes. By God, had I known that they would act this way, I would have never done what I did earlier. I am ashamed of the misdeeds I have committed and come to you for repentance. I want to sacrifice myself, and I think that would serve the purpose of atonement." Ḥusayn very kindly invoked divine blessings on him and said, "May Allah accept your repentance and forgive you. Just as your mother named you, you are a free man and, God willing, you will remain free in both this world and the hereafter."

Al-Hurr Addresses the Enemy

Al-Hurr then addressed the enemies and said they should have accepted any of the conditions offered by Ḥusayn so that God might save them from an ordeal. They said that his question would be answered by their commander 'Umar ibn Sa'd. 'Umar said that he himself wished to accept his offer, but his proposal was rejected. Thereafter, al-Hurr made a passionate speech and put the Kufans to shame for breaking their promise. In reply, they started shooting arrows.

Al-Hurr was forced to return to the camp.

The Battle Starts

When Ḥusayn's sincere efforts to bring round the enemy failed, confrontation became inevitable. He had only seventy-two followers in all, the enemy outnumbering his army in both men and resources. According to the old tradition of war, a single warrior came forward challenging his rival and then started the fight.

Later on, a full-fledged battle ensued. In the beginning, resistance by Ḥusayn's army was very effective, but they could not maintain it for long due to the enemy's numerical supremacy. Ḥusayn's supporters, relatives and youthful and younger sons were killed after playing a heroic role in the battle. Eventually, Ḥusayn remained alone to face the grim situation single-handed.

Sinan Ibn Anas Kills Ḥusayn

Now the time of Ḥusayn's martyrdom had arrived. Zur'a ibn Sharik al-Tamimi injured Ḥusayn's left hand and then dealt a blow to his shoulder. Ḥusayn swerved due to weakness. Frightened, the men from the enemy's side moved to the rear. Sinan ibn Anas of

Najaf came forward and attacked Ḥusayn with a spear. Ḥusayn fell down. Then he asked a person who was standing by to separate his head from the body. He rushed but had no courage to do it. Sinan ibn Anas, indignant, cursed him, dismounted from his horse and cut off Ḥusayn's head.

Ja'far ibn Muḥammad ibn 'Alī narrates that thirty-three injuries and thirty-four wounds were inflicted on his body with spears and swords, respectively.

The Duty of Ḥusayn's Followers

These are the details of a centuries-old tragic event, the importance of which cannot be underestimated. Even if they are ignored, the days of Muharram that recur every year keep this paramount tragedy afresh in our memory. But how many people are there who view this great tragedy in the right perspective and clearly grasp its meaning for continuing struggle between good and evil in the world. This is, indeed, a magnificent sacrifice that has gone a long way in consolidating and stabilising truth. A person who claims to be a devoted follower of Ḥusayn should always be ready to follow his example and exert himself for justice and truth in his limited sphere.

Everything in this material world is perishable,

but a martyr always remains a living source of inspiration to all good and just people.

The Nature of the Umayyad Rule

To illustrate a few points, it may here be stated that the Umayyad's rule was un-Islamic. Any rule s based on force and violence can never be Islamic. The Umayyads crushed the spirit of democratic freedom. They laid the foundation of their authority on unscrupulous tactics and coercive methods instead of on mutual consultation and consensus. The Umayyad state-craft did not follow the divine *sharia* in its totality but was motivated merely by lust for power and political ends. Such a serious menace to the basic values of Islam demanded a heroic struggle against arbitration and a crusade for the vindication of truth and freedom.

Ḥusayn's Role

Ḥusayn, Prince of Martyrs, initiated a holy war against the oppressive regime of the Umayyads and refused to pledge allegiance to that authority. It is a sacred legacy bequeathed to posterity by Ḥusayn that Muslims should never submit to any authority that defies divine law, maintains itself by force and foists its arbitrary decisions on the people at the cost of inherent human freedom. The struggle in this cause does not necessitate mobilisation of men, money or material on the scale possessed by the hostile temporal authority. Ḥusayn ibn ʻAlī did not possess the sinews of war. He had the support of only a small band of helpless and unarmed individuals. A person entrenched in righteousness and truth does not care for consequences. The outcome of the struggle lies in the hands of the power that is always on the side of justice and truth. Cruelty eventually suffers a setback and gains despair and despondency despite its overwhelming superiority in number and resources. On such occasions, one surrenders to considerations of expediency through the agency of the accursed Devil who creates doubt in the minds of the defenders of truth as to whether the outcome is worth achieving at the cost of much bloodshed. This can very easily be contradicted. Apart from numerous instances of *jihād*, there is the event of Karbala, which is a glaring example of a fight heroically fought by sixty-two to seventy-two scantily armed people against the massive forces of a formidable state. It is true that Ḥusayn saw his kith and kin in utter distress, suffering the agonies of hunger and thirst, witnessed each and every one of them writhing in dust and blood one after the other. It is also a fact that he did not even possess the force to wrest a morsel of bread from the enemy sufficient for their survival, but he eventually surrendered himself to the Supreme Being, sustaining grave injuries all over his body. However, he came out from the test triumphant. His wounded head was adored with the crown of victory.

Repercussions to Ḥusayn's Martyrdom

His body, no doubt, writhed in dust and blood, but each drop of his blood that gushed out from his wounds and flowed on the rocks and sands of Karbala caused fiery revolutions that could not be resisted by the bloodthirsty sword of Muslim ibn 'Uqba. Neither the brutality of al-Ḥajjāj nor the statesmanship of 'Abd al-Mālik were able to put a stop to it. The revolution continued to prevail far and wide for a long time. Atrocities of these kings added fuel to the fire. The governmental pride and arrogance caused the ashes to develop into a conflagration. Eventually, the time for natural retaliation arrived. Whatever had happened at Karbala in 62 AH was repeated in 132 AH, not only in Damascus but throughout the Islamic world. The heads that once wore the crown, and the people who had once adorned the throne, were seen rolling in dust and blood. Their bodies were crushed under horses' hoofs. The conquerors exhumed their graves and their remains were dug out completely. The Qur'anic verse "*The evildoers will find out what they will return to*" (al-Shu'arā 26:227) manifested itself in all aspects.

All that had taken place was only the outcome of Ibrahim 'Abbasi's activities and secret conspiracies plotted by Abu Muslim of Khurasan. Was that not the reaction to Ḥusayn's murder, was committed on the bank of the Euphrates? These were really the after-effects of sacrifices made for the vindication of truth that emerges sooner or later.

Morals of Ḥusayn's Performance

Ḥusayn's exemplary conduct teaches us not to care for consequences. If the temporal authority is aggressive, sacrifice on the part of the followers of truth becomes all the more essential. The numerical minority or majority or the lack of resources should not deter them from continuing their struggle. The grandeur of a coercive government does not carry the seal of divine approval that it should necessarily be obeyed. A truth-loving person has to face an oppressor whether weak or strong. Adherence to truth and justice is, no doubt, an ordeal. At every step, there are diversions due to an attachment to one's own life, honour and family. But Ḥusayn's lofty ideal teaches the believers and sincere Muslims that at the very outset, they should take stock of the strength of their resoluteness so that these temptations do not prove a stumbling block immediately after embarking on that mission. Everyone knows that in the presence of various attachments, the great martyr of Karbala sacrificed his all at the altar of truth. All the stages of ordeals were there for a test. These stages of ordeals are categorically described in the Holy Qur'an. Allah intends to test the believers by bringing them under the throes of various ordeals:

> "*Surely we will try you with some fear and hunger and loss of wealth, lives and crops; but give glad tidings to the steadfast, who say, when a misfortune strikes them, 'Surely we are Allah's, and surely to Him we are returning.*" (al-Baqarah 2:155-156)

Fear and apprehension, hunger and thirst, love of wealth, property, life and progeny form an acid test for human beings, and, as such, the sacrifice of these interests have been declared an ordeal in the cause of Allah.

The helpless hero of Karbala had all these stages, at a stretch. He could have got rid of them within a short span of time and secured relief, position and grandeur, had he only made a compromise with the aggressive government ignoring the dictates of truth and justice. Ḥusayn preferred Allah's will to his own personal choice. Devotion to truth overcomes love for life and its luxuries. He laid down his life, the only asset with the lover of Truth, but he never extended in allegiance his hand, which could be extended only in the cause of truth.

The most valuable lesson that can be deduced from this grave event is perseverance and determination in the path of *jihād* and truth.

In spite of being helplessly besieged by the enemy, with his family members, relatives and friends, witnessing his own kith and kin wailing *and* shrieking with the intensity of thirst and hunger, and later lifting with his own hands their bodies stained with blood, Ḥusayn never swerved an inch from the path of truth, even for a moment. In short, he underwent these calamities, tacitly grateful to Allah. Those who are surcharged with the intoxication of devotion and love willingly accept a cup of poison from the hands of their friend in preference to a cup of honey and elixir. Even today, every dust particle in Karbala gives a lesson in patience and endurance to those who keep their ears open to listen to its message.

Notes

[1] *Al-Tabari* and *al-Kamil.*

[2] *Al-Tabari* and *al-Kamil.*

[3] Ibid.

[4] Ibid.

[5] *Al-Imama wa al-Siyasa.*

[6] *Al-Tabari* and *al-Kamil.*

[7] Ibn Jarir.

[8] *Al-Tabari* and *al-Ya'qubi.*

[9] *Al-Tabari* and *al-Kamil.*

[10] *Al-Ya'qubi* and *al-Tabari.*

[11] Ibid.

[12] Al-Tabari.

CHAPTER FOUR

The Spirit of Ḥusayn's Martyrdom

Zakir Husain Khan

In this vast and wide universe, godly people of all castes and creeds have always displayed unity in diversity. It is undeniable that truth is one and only one. But observers visualise it in their own perspectives with the capacity they possess and voice their feelings in their own way. If a message is to be conveyed in the form it is intelligible to people of all communities professing different faiths and designed to leave a lasting impression on them, it becomes imperative to speak in the common language, avoiding terms and phraseology peculiar to different religious denominations. As far as I conceive, the main object of writing on Ḥusayn's martyrdom is to upraise and evaluate his performance in accordance with generally accepted criteria and explain it from an objective standpoint. If, however, prospective listeners are prepared to lend their ears with sympathy and devotion, even a hint or suggestion will serve the purpose.

Ḥusayn's Martyrdom and Humanity

Now questions arise as to whether Ḥusayn's martyrdom was only the result of his attempt to seize the throne and the sympathy it evokes in readers is the natural reaction to a splendid failure; whether this was merely the recalcitrant attitude or unscrupulous policy of a short-tempered leader who, by chance, happened to be their beloved Prophet's ﷺ grandson and, solely on this account, they came out in his defence; whether this is a heart-rending story of the ruthless and brutal destruction of a weak party, the narration of which induces you to burst into tears.

The history of the world provides a number of instances appealing to our sympathy. It is so replete with individual and collective incidents of failure and frustration on one hand, and those of cruelty and barbarism on the other, that the world will not be particularly impressed by the tragic episode of

Ḥusayn. No! Ḥusayn's story does not purport to be anything of this kind. It is, in the main, a story of human dignity, a tale revealing the essential nobility of man, an account of man's ascent to the peak of grandeur. It presents a lofty ideal of individual and collective human life; it is a milestone in the long journey from beastly slavery to human freedom; it is a proclamation of God's kingdom in this ephemeral world; it is an irrefutable proof of the possibility of its establishment among human beings; it is a beacon that guides humanity to perfection.

Whenever evil forces make a bid to put out this light with their mouths, Ḥusayn's monumental performance intensifies its refulgence. When humanity falters in adhering to the path of truth and freedom, the example set by Ḥusayn gives it support and comes to its rescue. When the tyrants proud of their wealth, power and authority harass the unassuming and helpless followers of truth, and when the incessant failure of the champions of truth cast doubt on the validity of its claim, Ḥusayn's heroic stand in its cause teaches them the lesson of perseverance and saves them from falling prey to despair and despondency. When the rising power of tyrants overawes the individual, Ḥusayn's example reminds him that the duty of stimulating resistance against brutal power ultimately devolves on him. It matters not if, for making such an attempt, the enemy offers him a cup of poison, sends him to the gallows, stones him to death or stains the earth with his blood. To worldly people, Ḥusayn brings home the fact that life does not mean just living. He asserts that life sometimes means to live and sometimes to surrender it.

When the golden calf of "imperialist power" becomes the object of worship everywhere, the name of frustrated Ḥusayn dispels the magic of Samari (maker of the golden calf) and, on that occasion, the victory of the followers of falsehood pales into insignificance when compared to Ḥusayn's failure in the cause of truth.

Ḥusayn's Dignity and its Secret

What is all this for? Because Ḥusayn has, by sacrificing his life, testified to the fact that God is the supreme authority of the world, and that man is more dignified than other creatures of the universe. He affixed a seal to this truth with his blood.

What is meant by man's "dignity"? What makes man superior to beasts and animals? His intuitive perception of laws and morals; his advancement from good to better; his heart's eagerness for higher values; his natural inclination to move from inferior to superior; his inherent abhorrence to be content with lowly things, being conscious of higher aims and objectives; and his full and implicit faith in high ideals and ratification of these values with his heart and conscience. Moral values such as justice, truth, virtue and beauty are the qualities based on which the value of each and every thing is appraised.

By virtue of these attributes, man's life becomes meaningful, his discontent disappears, his agitated heart is solaced and he is guided to the right path if he goes astray. These remind him of *ahsan al-taqwim* (the best stature) in the abysmal pit of *asfal al-safilin* (the lowest of the low). If forgotten, they call on the memory repeatedly. Even if crushed, they emerge time and again. These absolute values are not perceived by senses. They can only be approached through imagination. The naked eye cannot catch their vision; only insight can catch a glimpse of them. There are, in every part of the world, righteous people who witness these values unveiled, just as we see the moon, the sun and the stars. With the help of this light, they wish to illuminate everything in the universe, every sphere of human life, both individually and collectively. They proclaim these higher values by their precept and confirm them by their practice. They are one with them. They absorb them in their selves. Thus, with the radiance of their pious lives, they persuade others to acquaint themselves with those ideals and to dedicate themselves to their realisation. When the forces of evil rush on them suddenly, they gird up their loins for defence. While defending them, they, no doubt, often come out victorious, but their glory is exhibited more brilliantly in the case of discomfort. Their success does strengthen belief in these values, but this belief is still more strengthened in cases where truth has apparently failed. Even though quite sure of failure, the seekers of truth do not join hands with the opposition group betraying the higher values. In return, they suffer abuse, face humiliation and undergo persecution. If destined to enjoy the highest privilege, they eventually give an outright proof of their adherence to truth by laying down their lives and impress on humanity that their loyalty to higher values is not conditional on their success and that, even in failure and defeat, they will remain steadfast in their devotion to truth. No, failure as a result of adherence to these principles is more valuable than victory achieved in the company of others.

Pursuit of a high ideal, even at the cost of popularity is preferable to the pursuit of an ignoble but popular objective. Adherence to a sublime ideal, even if it is unsuccessful, is more worthy of respect than success achieved in the pursuit of an ignoble end. The gloomy loneliness of a selfless worker in a noble cause is better than the support of a huge army in gaining an aim low in the scale of value. Ḥusayn was the torchbearer of absolute values. He lived, fought and sacrificed his life in the defence of these ideals. He lit an ever-lasting beacon for humanity by his heroic struggle for truth and righteousness, which could not be extinguished even after his death. The glorious example of his life enables mankind to purify social life and checks the evil that brings corruption into the body politic. This light is a source of guidance in every walk of human life.

Discrimination Between Truth and Falsehood

According to Islam, religion is based on unity of values. Authority, wisdom and truth are fundamental values. Wisdom and truth are well-known basic values. Here I want to elucidate the meaning of *authority*. It means "government that wields supreme authority". If you give consideration to this point for a moment, the fact will come to light that the best political organisation for human beings and the establishment of a government based on equity and justice are essential for moulding the moral life of human society. From this, it follows that a moral value is one of the constituents of a good government. A full-fledged pattern of such a government is as much required for our guidance as wisdom and truth. This is called authority. Submission to authority and devotion to wisdom and truth are enjoined by Islam. To put it in other words, Islam says that authority emanates from the Supreme Being who is the source of truth and wisdom. Worship (*i.e.* unconditional obedience) is due only to Him and none else. The others may also be obeyed, subject to certain conditions. One condition is that temporal authority should not run counter to divine authority, wisdom and truth.

If divine authority is established in this world, a man is bound to obey it unconditionally. In the case of temporal authority, submission to it will be subject to certain conditions. The first and foremost condition is that a person should not act against the dictates of divine authority. A man faces a grim situation, indeed, when the commands of temporal authority are at variance with those of divine authority and he is forced to obey them. A more serious position is created, the very imagination of which makes the heart of truth-seekers shiver, when secular authority demands that it should be treated as absolute authority. When such a calamity overtakes the world, it becomes the duty of a truth-seeker to declare, by word and deed, that the commands of secular authority are absolutely contrary to divine authority and that he would never bow before it, nor should anyone else surrender to it. This declaration is known as bearing witness to truth. The person who makes this declaration is assailed by all the evil forces. It is only by contending against these forces that a truth-seeker can bring home to mankind the basic difference between truth and un-truth.

I have just stated that there are very few who can see the higher values unveiled. Now the question is how a truth-seeker who has a clear vision of truth can communicate it to others who are not reckoned so fortunate. The only alternative left for him is to win over their hearts by sacrifice in the cause of truth. Sometimes, he is called on to sacrifice even his life. Only that person who adheres to truth till the last moment at the risk of his life attains the highest stage of martyrdom and is called a martyr.

Fight Against Falsehood

Turn over the pages of history! The early period of Islam, considered the best, has elapsed. Even the period of the true successors to the Prophet ﷺ was terminated. The age of secular authority—the period of autocratic government—has been ushered in. In flagrant contravention to divine authority, Muslim kings look on the state treasury as their personal property. In each Muslim state, the monarch fills his treasury with gold and jewellery. With his political power reinforced by the power of money, he forces the people to obey his arbitrary commands. Some people submit to him out of fear, and others do so to gain their selfish ends with his help.

There is always a hard core of steadfast Muslims who refuse to yield. The Prophet's ﷺ grandson Ḥusayn is one of them. Persuasion, threats and crafty measures were employed, but Ḥusayn remained adamant. How could Ḥusayn—in whose veins the blood of 'Alī, Fatima and Muḥammad was pulsating, who was God-fearing, who had devotion to truth—treat falsehood on par with truth? Ḥusayn flatly refused to pledge allegiance to Yazīd. In effect, Ḥusayn declared that Yazīd's authority, which was in conflict with divine authority, should not be obeyed by true Muslims. This was the first step in the direction of martyrdom.

He was driven out of his native place. He could not live in peace even in Mecca. He, therefore, resolved to migrate to Iraq. This amounted to a proclamation, on his part, that Yazīd's claim to authority in the Muslim state was untenable. The idea of submitting to Yazīd was so repugnant to him that he decided to renounce the security and comforts of his homeland. This was the second step leading to martyrdom.

On his way to Kufa, in Karbala, Ḥusayn was intercepted by Yazīd's forces. The small band of his followers was surrounded by Yazīd's army. This was the last sacrifice and the final ordeal. He successfully passed the test. Each and every one of his relatives and companions was killed one after another. Children were slain. Finally, Ḥusayn himself, a mass of wounds and bruises, fell from his horse. His heart harboured and his lips uttered the belief that "there is no object of worship except Allah, and absolute authority is vested in Him alone." This was martyrdom, the sacrifice of one's life for the vindication of truth. Thirteen centuries have since elapsed, yet the example set by Ḥusayn gives and will continue to give till eternity evidence that command rests with Allah.

Wherever divine authority is respected, men will remember how the grandson of the greatest benefactor of humanity sacrificed his life in the defence of truth. In the future, when, with the increase of human knowledge, obstacles to progress would be removed and people would march confidently to the goal of self-realisation, they would surely recall the glorious sacrifice offered by Ḥusayn at the altar of truth. When the human mind will be rid of every fear except the fear of God, Ḥusayn will be accorded the respect he deserves and people will often think how Fatima's beloved son displayed the sublimity of obedience to Allah by the voluntary sacrifice of his life. Then alone would this helpless man come into prominence as the ruler of rulers. This frustrated man will be regarded as the custodian of religion and faith. Once covered with blood and dust, his head will become the symbol of absolute submission to divine authority and fearless defiance of any other type of temporal power.

CHAPTER FIVE

Implications of Ḥusayn's Sacrifice

Abul Alā Mawdūdī

Every year, in the month of Muharram, millions of Muslims mourn Ḥusayn's martyrdom. It is regrettable that among these mourners, there are very few people who focus their attention on the cause for which Ḥusayn not only sacrificed his own life, but also the lives of his kith and kin. It is but natural for the relatives and devoted followers of a man to feel grieved at his martyrdom. This sort of sentiment does not carry much moral value; it is nothing but a spontaneous reaction of his relatives' and sympathisers' minds. But the point at issue is the special feature that keeps the grief for Ḥusayn afresh, although 1,300 years have elapsed since this tragic event.

If the martyrdom is not associated with any high ideal, it is meaningless to say that the mourning continues for centuries merely on personal grounds. If viewed in correct perspective, one may well ask what value Ḥusayn himself would attach to such devotion. If his own person were dearer to him than any ideology or object, why did he sacrifice it at all? His sacrifice is a conclusive proof that this object was dearer to him than his own life. If we do not have a clear idea of Ḥusayn's purpose, but continue our lamentation at each anniversary of his martyrdom, neither can we expect any appreciation from Ḥusayn on Resurrection Day, nor will it have any value with his God.

Let us ask what that ideal or object was! Did Ḥusayn affirm his claim to succession to the caliphate and did he stake his life to vindicate this claim? Anyone who knows the high moral standard of Ḥusayn's household cannot harbour this vile notion that the members of such a sacred family could have caused bloodshed among the Muslims for gaining political power for themselves. If, for argument's sake, this viewpoint takes for granted that members of Banu Hashim had a claim for power, even then the fifty-year history, from Abū Bakr's caliphate down to the period of Mu'āwiya, bears evidence that waging war and causing bloodshed merely to seize power had never been their motive.

As a logical conclusion, one has to admit that Ḥusayn's keen eye discerned symptoms of decay and corruption in the system of the Islamic state, and he felt compelled to resist these evil forces. He even deemed it his duty to wage war in this connection, as the situation so warranted.

Change in the Nature and Object of Constitution

What was that imminent change? People had not apparently deviated from their religion. All the people including the ruling class had faith in God, the Prophet ﷺ and the Holy Qur'an as they did in the past. There was no change in the state laws either. The courts of judicature of the Umayyad state continued to decide cases according to the injunctions laid down in the Qur'an and *Sunnah* in the manner they were decided during the period prior to the Umayyad's seizure of power. As a matter of fact, no legal change ever took place in any Muslim state in the world before the nineteenth century.

Some people talk of Yazīd's personal character, highlighting its dark side. This has naturally given rise to a common assumption that the stand taken by Ḥusayn was that a person with the reprehensible character of Yazīd should not be allowed to continue as the head of the Islamic state. But in spite of admitting the worst possible picture of Yazīd's personal character, it is not correct to say that this alone would have instigated Ḥusayn to rebellion against the constituted authority, especially when state administration was functioning on a sound basis. The personal factor was not by itself responsible for Ḥusayn's mental perturbation. The fact that comes to light after a deep study of history is that Yazīd's nomination as his father's successor and later his coronation as king actually marked a radical change in the object and conduct of the Islamic constitution. Although the consequences of this change were not disclosed at that time, in its entirety a farsighted person could easily apprehend, at the very outset, where the change would lead. At first glance, Ḥusayn foresaw the catastrophe towards which the Islamic state was heading and resolved to stake his life for its prevention.

Point of Deviation

In order to fully understand this situation, we have to find out the characteristic feature of the constitution that had been guiding the state administration for a period of forty years under the leadership of the Prophet ﷺ and his rightly guided successors. Further, what were the main features of the administrative system of a new Muslim state taking birth under the aegis of the Umayyad, Abbasid and subsequent dynasties right up from the time of Yazīd's nomination. From this comparative study, we will be able to distinguish between the courses—one adopted by the early Muslim state and the other by the subsequent states till they reached the point of deviation. From this study, we will also know why a person who was brought up and trained under the direct guidance of the Prophet ﷺ, Fatima and 'Alī, and who enjoyed the best society of the Prophet's ﷺ Companions from his infancy to the middle age, took the stand of resisting the new change, irrespective of consequences, when the point of deviation was setting in.

Beginning of Monarchism

Mere oral assent to the following propositions is not enough:

1. Sovereignty of the Muslim state is wholly vested in the Supreme Being.
2. People are His subjects.

3. Rulers are accountable to Allah.
4. The conduct of the individual and the state should be determined by this doctrine.

The first and the foremost feature of the Islamic state is that a person should have implicit faith in Allah and it should be clearly understood that government has no absolute power over the subjects, nor are the subjects its slaves. The rulers should first enrol themselves as Allah's slaves. Next, they have to implement divine law among their subjects.

Yazīd's nomination as successor to his father Mu'āwiya marked the beginning of that type of monarchy, in which mere oral assent to Allah's sovereignty was demanded of individuals. In practice, like all former monarchs, Muslim rulers behaved as if they were the sole repository of sovereignty, that sovereignty is vested in the monarch and his legitimate successors. The monarch was supposed to be the undisputed master of life, property, honour and everything belonging to his subjects. Divine law, if enforced in his territory, was intended only for the common man. Kings themselves violated many provisions of divine law with impunity and the nobles were also tempted to follow suit.

Neglecting the Moral Obligation to Enjoin Right and Forbid Wrong

The main object of the Islamic state was to establish and promote the virtues chosen by Allah as well as to prevent and suppress vices disliked by Him, while the object of autocratic government was no other than grabbing land, self-aggrandisement, collection of tribute and gratification of sensual desires. The monarchs were rarely inclined to vindicate the cause of truth and justice. Kings, their nobles and their officials were instrumental in propagating vice rather than virtue. Most of the godly people who contributed their might to the promotion of good and suppression of vice, preaching Islam, compiling books on religion and carrying on research in Islamic studies, incurred the displeasure of rulers and were hardly ever patronised. These virtuous people, however, continued to adhere to their mission in spite of opposition from state authorities. Contrary to the efforts of these scholars and pious people, the lifestyles and policies of the rulers, officers and their subordinates continuously led Muslim society to moral degradation. They even went to the extreme of creating obstacles in the propagation of Islam to achieve their nefarious end. The worst example of this practice is found in the imposition of tax (*jizya*) on converted Muslims during the Umayyad period.

Righteousness and fear of God are at the heart of the Islamic faith. These noble qualities should be reflected in the character of the Islamic head of state. Government employees, judges and military officers imbibed this spirit and, in turn, infused it into Muslim society. The moment Muslim rulers and government adopted the pomp and pageantry of Caesar, suppression and high-handedness continued to be practised in place of justice. Profligacy and luxury had come into vogue. The rulers failed to distinguish between lawful and unlawful. Political policy was no longer coherent with morality. The officials kept the people under their own control instead of developing fear of God within themselves. They won over the people through temptation and bribery instead of awakening their conscience.

Fundamental Principles of the Islamic Constitution

Such was the deplorable change in the spirit, purpose and character of Muslim rulers. A similar change appeared also in the fundamental principles of the Islamic constitution. Each of the following seven important principles underwent a thorough transformation:

1. Free Election

Formation of government with free consent of the people is the cornerstone of the Islamic constitution. Nobody should employ force to secure power for himself. People should entrust power to the best among the candidates after consultation among themselves. Everyone should be free to pledge allegiance or to refuse to do so. There should be no maneuvering to secure this oath of fealty. People should be quite free in this regard. Unless the oath of allegiance is secured, no one should seize power; and when people lose confidence in him, he should not stick to power any longer. Each of the true successors to the Prophet ﷺ came to power according to this prescribed procedure. In the absence of these conditions, Muʿāwiya had only a dubious claim to succession. This is the reason why he was not included among the true successors although he himself would claim to be one of the Prophet's ﷺ Companions.

Yazīd's nomination as his successor was a high-handed reactionary act that abrogated the constitutional provision and resulted in hereditary monarchy. Ever since the law governing the election of the caliph remained in abeyance, clever and wealthy people managed to seize power instead of being freely elected by the Muslim community. Allegiance was secured through power instead of securing power through voluntary allegiance. People were not free in the matter of pledging allegiance. Securing allegiance had no longer been a prerequisite of acquiring power. In the first place, people had no courage to refuse allegiance to the person who possessed power. If at all the people refused allegiance, the person who had already come to power did not part with it. When Imam Mālik, during the reign of the Abbasid caliph al-'Abbasi, committed the "offence" of asking the caliph to abstain from coercively securing allegiance, he was flogged and his arms were dislocated from his shoulders.

2. Advisory System

Another important article of this constitution is the establishment of an advisory system of government. Advice of learned, pious people and those of sound judgment enjoying confidence of the people should be sought. During the period of the first four caliphs, members of the advisory council were not elected. They were men who enjoyed the right to vote by the tacit consent of the people. It cannot be said, by any stretch of the imagination, that an aspirant to the caliphate had selected them because he knew that he would support him. As a matter of fact, they chose the best people from the community with all sincerity and disinterest. They were expected to speak out the truth and express their opinion according to the dictates of their conscience with precision and integrity. There was not the least doubt that they would permit the ruler to go astray. Had the elections been held at that time in accordance with the existing technique, Muslims in general would have reposed confidence in the same people only. With the advent of the monarchy, the advisory system underwent a total transformation. The monarchical administration was based on autocratic and despotic methods. The princes, sycophants, courtiers, provincial governors and military commanders served in the council as members. Only those people assumed advisory positions who, if an opinion poll had been taken, would have scored thousands of votes of censure against one vote of confidence. On the contrary, truth-loving, learned and God-fearing people who enjoyed public confidence had no value in the eyes of the despotic rulers. They rather incurred the kings' wrath or were viewed by them at least with suspicion.

3. Freedom of Opinion

The third article of the constitution provides for freedom of opinion. Furtherance of virtue and suppression of evils have been enjoined by Islam not only as the right of Muslims, but as their essential duty. Freedom of conscience and speech was the pivot on which Islamic society and the state administration functioned in the right direction. People must have the liberty to find fault with the most prominent among Muslims in case they went astray, and be outspoken in all matters. During the tenure of the four caliphs, not only were people's rights perfectly safe, but the caliphs also regarded it as their duty and encouraged people to discharge such duty. Freedom of speech, giving a warning and demanding an explanation from the caliph himself were not restricted only to the members of the advisory council, but were also enjoyed by each and every individual Muslim. If they exercised this right, they were not taken to task. On the other hand, their bold step was extolled and applauded. This freedom was not a gift of the ruler, but a constitutional right bestowed on them by Islam, and they regarded it as their duty to pay it due respect. The use of this privilege for the vindication of the right was an obligation entrusted to every Muslim by God and His Messenger ﷺ. Keeping the atmosphere of the society and state congenial for the fulfilment of this obligation was considered to be an integral part of the caliphate's functions.

With the domination of kings, the voice of conscience was stifled and freedom of speech was totally denied. A trend that developed during that period was that if anyone had to speak, he should speak in favour of the ruler and the government, or else he must maintain silence. If the urge of conscience was so powerful that one could not desist from declaring the truth, he had to be prepared for the loss of freedom or life. This state of affairs had an adverse effect on the moral of the general public. Muslims became discouraged, cowards and time-servers. The number of people who could risk their lives by adhering to truth began to diminish. Flattery loomed large in society. Truth-loving people had no value at all. Highly-qualified and honest people with independent views severed their connections with the government. People disliked the government so much that they felt no desire to maintain it. When a new party emerged to displace the old one, people never moved their little finger in support of the latter. One regime succeeded another. People witnessed the in-coming and out-going spectacle as passive spectators without evincing any interest therein.

4. Sense of Responsibility to God and His Creation

The fourth article, which has a close affinity with the preceding one, was that both the caliph and his government were responsible before Allah. As far as the sense of this responsibility is concerned, it kept the four true caliphs restless day and night. Each of them considered himself accountable for their words and deeds before God and the people. It was not necessary that the caliph should be questioned in the parliament only after raising a call attention motion. They faced the public five times a day in the congregational prayer in the mosque. Every Friday, the caliphs acquainted the public with the affairs of the state and also gave them a hearing. They moved about in the marketplace without being escorted by a bodyguard and mixed with the people unprotected by a security force.

The portals of the government house (which was only an ordinary structure) were always kept open, and every visitor had free access to the caliphs. On all such occasions, everyone could meet them, make a query and ask for their explanation. They had to be ready to be questioned by anyone at any time. The right to question the caliph was not restricted to the representatives alone, but enjoyed and exercised by every Muslim. They assumed power with the consent of the people, who were the supreme authority competent to remove a caliph and elect another in his place. The elected caliph did not, therefore, anticipate any danger in meeting the people. They were not even afraid of being removed from the office.

The imperialist regime was totally devoid of the concept of responsible government. For them, the responsibility to Allah was only an oral assent and it was rarely translated into action. As for the responsibility to the people, nobody had the courage to ask for an explanation from them. They exercised absolute authority over the people. They had acquired power by dint of force and, as such, challenged anybody to wrest power from their hands, if he could do so. How could such people face the public, and how could the public have access to such people? Even when they offered prayer, it was done either in well-guarded mosques in a special locality or in an open place generally surrounded by their close associates. Whenever they went out in vehicles, they had an armed police entourage both in front and behind to keep the way clear of traffic. There was scarcely any chance of their coming across the public.

5. Bayt al-Mal, a Trust

The fifth article of the Islamic constitution laid down that *bayt al-mal* (the public treasury) was Allah's property and a trust with the Muslims. Nothing should be received except through lawful sources, and nothing should go out except for lawful purposes. The caliph enjoyed only as much jurisdiction over it as a trustee has over the property of a minor orphan under his custody:

> "*Whoever is rich, let him abstain altogether, and whoever is poor, let him eat reasonably.*" (al-Nisā' 4:6)

The caliph was bound to account for the income and expenditure of *bayt al-mal*, and the Muslims had every right to ask the caliph for a full account of income and expenditure.

The rightly-guided caliphs meticulously followed this principle. Whatever was deposited in the treasury was deposited according to Islamic law, and expenditure was met on correct lines. Whoever was well-to-do among them performed honorary services without drawing a single penny from *bayt al-mal* towards his remuneration. Moreover, he never hesitated to spend from his own pocket in the interest of the nation. Those who could not afford to serve without emoluments took the minimum to meet their essential requirements of life. Every reasonable person would admit that the remuneration they took was far less than what was actually due. Even a hostile critic would not dare contradict this. Every Muslim had the right to demand the accounts of the income and expenditure of the public treasury, and the caliphs were always prepared to explain. A common man had the right to ask, "How was he able to prepare such a lengthy tunic for himself when the dimensions of cloths from Yemen could not make one of so big a size?"

When the caliphate degenerated into autocracy, the public treasury became exclusively the private property of the king instead of being divine or public property. Money was received both through lawful and unlawful sources and squandered in legal and illegal ways. Nobody had the courage to demand a statement of accounts. The entire revenue of the state was a source of enjoyment being exploited by everyone from an ordinary letter-bearer right up to the state administrator, according to his capability. They were completely unmindful of the fact that authority over administration was not a licence for misappropriating the public trust. They were fully convinced that they would continue to devour the public treasury and nobody would dare question them.

6. Rule of the Law

The sixth article of this Constitution contemplates the establishment of God's kingdom. Nobody should be over and above the law or transgress the limits demarcated by law. There should be uniform legal provisions for all—from a common man to the head of the state. It should be enforced on everyone without any discrimination. Partiality should not be allowed to intrude into matters of justice and equity. The courts of law should be free from outside pressure. The four caliphs had set up the best example of adhering to this principle. In spite of enjoying powers more than kings, they strictly adhered to divine law. Friendship and nepotism never induced the caliphs to ignore the prescribed rules and regulations, nor did their displeasure cause harm to any one against the cannons of Islamic law. If anyone happened to infringe their inherent right, they referred the matter to court just like a common man.

If someone had a complaint against them, his grievances were redressed in a court of law. Similarly, the governors and commanders-in-chief were held in the grip of the law. Nobody dared influence the judge in his favour in cases pending trial. Anyone who contravened the provisions of law had no chance of escaping the legal consequences. No sooner was the caliphate converted into monarchism than this Islamic ideology was consigned to oblivion. Not only were the kings, princes, nobles, officials and commanders above the law, but favourite valets and maidservants connected with the palace were as well. People were physically and morally at the mercy of state officials. There were two conflicting criteria to decide people's fate—one for the strong and the other for the weak. Pressure was brought to bear on the judges of the court. Those who observed integrity in deciding cases had to pay a heavy price for their integrity and scrupulous regard for justice. God-fearing jurists preferred undergoing torture and imprisonment to becoming instrumental in perpetrating aggression and high-handedness lest they fall a prey to divine chastisement

7. Full Equality in Rights and Status

The seventh article of the Islamic constitution pertains to full legal equality in rights and status. This was fully assured in the early period of the Islamic state. There was no discrimination among the Muslims based on race, language or place of birth. No one enjoyed superiority over another in view of his clan, family or race. There was uniformity in the rights of all who believed in Allah and His Messenger

ﷺ, and their status was determined based on equality. If preference was to be given, it was based on character, capability, aptitude and service. When the caliphate was replaced by imperialism, the demons of prejudice and bigotry became active (on all sides). The status of the members of the royal family and its supporters rose higher. The tribes related to the royal family were assigned a position of vantage over other tribes. Distinction between Arabs and non-Arabs was revived and struggle for power poisoned relations between Arab tribes. History bears witness to the extent of the damage caused by these factional wranglings.

Ḥusayn's Character as a Believer

These were the changes that appeared in the wake of converting the Islamic caliphate into dynastic imperialism. No one can deny that Yazīd's nomination as successor to his father was the starting point of all these transformations. It cannot be gainsaid that after a short span of time from the point of origin all the corrupt practices mentioned above came into existence. At the time when this revolutionary step was adopted, there was no indication of these evils, but a man of vision could have predicted these inevitable consequences of such a beginning, and that the reforms introduced by

Islam in the administration and political phases of the state would be rendered null and void by these changes. This is why Ḥusayn could not remain indifferent to this undesirable development. He, therefore, decided to stem the tide of the evil forces, taking the risk of confronting the worst consequences by rising in revolt against an established government. The consequences of his bold stand are known to everyone. The fact that Ḥusayn wanted to emphasise by plunging himself into grave danger and enduring its consequences heroically was that the fundamental features of the Islamic state are valuable assets. It would not be a bad bargain if a believer sacrificed his life and got his family members slain for preserving this valuable object. A believer should not hesitate to sacrifice all that he possesses for preventing the changes that constitute a serious danger to the religion of Islam and the Muslim community, which is a custodian of the constitutional values mentioned above. One is at liberty to contemptuously disregard it as merely a manoeuvre for securing power, but in the eyes of Ḥusayn ibn ʻAlī, it was primarily a religious obligation. He, therefore, laid down his life in this cause, gaining the crown of martyrdom.

Index

I

J

K

M

T

U

W

Y

Z

www.ingramcontent.com/pod-product-compliance
Ingram Content Group UK Ltd.
Pitfield, Milton Keynes, MK11 3LW, UK
UKHW042015190726
13854UKWH00005B/2300